REGULATION OF
PHARMACEUTICAL
INNOVATION

Evaluative Studies

This series of studies seeks to bring about greater understanding and promote continuing review of the activities and functions of the federal government. Each study focuses on a specific program, evaluating its cost and efficiency, the extent to which it achieves its objectives, and the major alternative means—public and private—for reaching those objectives. Yale Brozen, professor of economics at the University of Chicago and an adjunct scholar of the American Enterprise Institute for Public Policy Research, is the director of the program.

REGULATION OF PHARMACEUTICAL INNOVATION

The 1962 amendments

Sam Peltzman

With a foreword by Yale Brozen

American Enterprise Institute for Public Policy Research
Washington, D. C.

This study is one of a series published by the American Enterprise Institute as part of the research program of AEI's Center for Health Policy Research. A distinguished advisory committee, whose members are listed below, helps guide this program.

ISBN 0-8447-3128-5

Evaluative Studies 15, June 1974

Second printing, April 1975

Third printing, February 1978

Library of Congress Catalog Card No. L.C. 74-79250

CONTENTS

FOREWORD

How can any one quarrel with a requirement that a new drug must be shown, to the satisfaction of a government agency, to have the curative powers its producer claims for it before it can be sold? But that is what this study does.

Professor Peltzman did not set out to criticize this requirement when he undertook this study. He intended to measure the net benefits produced by the 1962 amendments to the Food, Drug, and Cosmetic Act—the amendments that instituted the efficacy requirement. In order to produce a result as favorable as possible to the 1962 amendments, he has made assumptions, where assumptions are necessary, which result in an overstatement of benefits and an understatement of costs. He has assumed, for example, that unsafe drugs will be kept off the market by the added information required of manufacturers to prove efficacy but that they would not have been kept off by the pre-1962 requirements of the law. (Under the law before it was amended, a marketer of a new drug had to prove to the satisfaction of the Food and Drug Administration [FDA] that his proposed new drug was safe for human consumption.) Professor Peltzman has made this assumption despite the fact that drugs such as thalidomide, which is safe except for use by pregnant women, had in fact been kept from being marketed under the proof-of-safety requirements existing before the 1962 amendments were passed. By making this assumption, he has attributed to the amendments benefits that might have occurred without the amendments.

Examining the delay in marketing of new drugs caused by the regulations instituted at the end of 1962, he has found evidence that an additional four years of testing is now required to provide the information necessary to file a New Drug Application (NDA) beyond

1

the two years of testing previously needed. Moreover, an additional two years of FDA processing of applications beyond the previous processing time has become the rule. Professor Peltzman has used a minimum estimate of only two years of additional delay in the availability of a new drug as the delay caused by the 1962 amendments. This minimizes the period in which lives are lost that might have been saved, or morbidity is protracted that might have been cut short, if new drugs were marketed earlier. It minimizes his estimate of the "cost" of the 1962 amendments.

Despite these and a number of other assumptions favorable to the 1962 amendments, Professor Peltzman is unable to find that the amendments have been beneficial. He finds instead a net cost equivalent to a tax of at least $300 million per year on the sick.

In the course of his investigation, Professor Peltzman comes to a number of conclusions on the effects of the 1962 amendments.

1. The number of new chemical entities (a new chemical useful in treating patients) reaching the market has been reduced by more than half as a result of the 1962 amendments. If it were mainly the inefficacious drugs whose marketing was prevented, we should expect a more than concomitant fall in the waste from expenditures on useless drugs or on new drugs no more useful than the old. Professor Peltzman finds no reduction in the incidence of waste from inefficacious drugs. What trifling reduction in waste has taken place could have occurred through a simple arbitrary limitation on the number of new drugs marketed.

2. In attempting to reduce the incidence of waste (an attempt which has failed), the FDA has required those who introduce new drugs to provide more information about any new drug than they had to provide before 1962 under the safety requirement of the unamended law. This has doubled the cost of developing and bringing a new drug to market. (Cost would have doubled in any case because of increased safety testing as a result of developments in pharmacological science, but actual real costs have quadrupled.) The increased cost and delay have greatly reduced the amount of drug innovation.

3. The major reason for the failure of the 1962 amendments to reduce the incidence of waste from expenditures on inefficacious drugs is that "the penalties imposed by the marketplace on sellers of ineffective drugs before 1962 seem to have been sufficient to have left little room for improvement by a regulatory agency." Ineffective drugs experience a substantial and fairly prompt loss of market share which makes it unprofitable to develop and launch such drugs. The same effort devoted to effective drugs is much more profitable.

4. Aside from the losses (in the form of deaths that might have been prevented and illnesses that might have been shortened) resulting from the lack of new drugs and the delays in introducing them, the 1962 amendments have imposed additional costs on consumers in the form of higher prices for drugs. Because of the decrease in the number of new drugs coming to market since 1962, prices of old drugs are higher than they otherwise would be. The higher prices for old drugs more than offset the premiums that would have been charged for new drugs if they had come to market. As a consequence the average of all drug prices is greater than it would have been if drug innovation had not been choked by the amendments. The reduced price competition results in the sick paying an estimated $50 million more each year for their prescriptions.

5. Although Professor Peltzman assumes that the additional information required by the 1962 amendments to satisfy the FDA's efficacy regulations may have prevented the marketing of some unsafe drugs, despite the requirement of proof of safety in the pre-1962 law, it may well be that doctors are forced to prescribe unsafe drugs for their patients which would have been replaced by safer drugs but for the 1962 amendments. Since the amendments greatly reduced the number of new drugs marketed and delayed the introduction of those that were, it is likely that some of the new drugs which would have been available but for the amendments would have provided greater safety than some of the old drugs on which doctors must rely. As Professor Peltzman reports, Dr. William Wardell has found that in the past decade improved drugs have been introduced in England which are not yet available in the United States, apparently because of the great cost and the delays involved in satisfying FDA requirements. Professor Wardell estimates, for example, that a drug available abroad for five years prior to its 1971 FDA approval for marketing in the United States could have saved 1,200 lives in the five years because it was safer than the only alternatives available prior to 1971 (see page 89). The net effect of the 1962 amendments, then, may well be more risk of adverse drug reactions and less safety than if the law had never been changed.

Graduate School of Business
University of Chicago   Yale Brozen

CHAPTER I

INTRODUCTION
AND SUMMARY

Increasingly frequent reports about the availability abroad of drugs that cannot be sold in the U.S. have brought pressure on the Food and Drug Administration (FDA) to defend its regulation of the marketing of new drugs. Some of the drugs which cannot be sold here are the drugs-of-choice for foreign physicians in the treatment of certain conditions. Their failure to win the FDA's approval for marketing here has provoked controversy among pharmacological experts. Further, the American rate of innovation in drugs has been lower following the passage of the landmark 1962 amendments to the Food, Drug and Cosmetic Act than it was before. Since these amendments established the framework of current FDA regulation of innovation, the extent to which this reduced rate of innovation can be attributed to the amendments has also been a matter of some controversy.

Inasmuch as the 1962 amendments were intended to prevent the marketing of some types of drugs, there may have been a net benefit from any regulatory-induced suppression of innovation. This study

This monograph summarizes the results of the author's research on the benefits and costs of new drug regulation, conducted under a grant from the Center for Policy Study, University of Chicago. These results were presented at the Conference on the Regulation of the Introduction of New Pharmaceuticals, sponsored by the center and held at the University of Chicago, December 4-5, 1972. The research results have subsequently been published in greater detail than in this monograph in *Regulating New Drugs,* ed. Richard Landau (University of Chicago: Center for Policy Study, 1973).

I am indebted to Yale Brozen, Harold Demsetz, Milton Friedman, James Jondrow, Richard Landau, and George Stigler for helpful comments and suggestions; to Joyce Iseri for diligent research assistance; and to Richard Burr and Paul de Haen of R. A. Gosselin, Inc. and Paul de Haen, Inc., respectively, for providing essential data.

tries to shed light on the way the 1962 amendments have worked in practice. Have they produced more benefits, by preventing the marketing of ineffective drugs and providing additional information about new drugs, than any losses they have imposed by, for example, suppressing potentially beneficial innovation?

Food and Drug Regulation

Federal regulation of the development and marketing of drugs goes back at least to the first decade of this century. The 1906 Food and Drug Act was the child of progressivism and of the legendary muckrakers. It was designed to protect consumers by requiring that a medicine's ingredients be stated on a package label. There was no important restriction on the content or use of drugs. Today's reader may find it curious that federal law deemed it adequate protection for the consumer if he simply knew "the quantity or proportion of any alcohol, morphine, opium, cocaine, heroin, . . . chloroform, cannabis . . . ," and so on, contained in a medicine.

This posture was modified in the Food, Drug and Cosmetic Act of 1938, passed in reaction to the introduction of a liquid form of the drug sulfanilamide, whose solvent was discovered to be a lethal poison after commercial distribution began. The 1938 law forbade marketing of any new drug until the Food and Drug Administration approved a New Drug Application (NDA) submitted by the manufacturer. Before approval was given, the NDA had to demonstrate that the drug was "safe" for the use suggested on the label. The law provided for automatic approval of any NDA not rejected within 180 days. In practice the FDA was able to extend this period by requests for further information.

The most recent important change in regulation of the development of new drugs came with the 1962 amendments to the 1938 law. The primary feature of the 1962 amendments is that a manufacturer must prove to the FDA's satisfaction that a drug has the curative powers the manufacturer claims for it. The costs and benefits of this requirement are the subject of this study.

The Kefauver Hearings

The initial impetus for changing the 1938 law came from hearings begun in 1959 by Senator Estes Kefauver's Antitrust and Monopoly Subcommittee. Underlying these hearings was a belief that prevailing regulation permitted the introduction of new drugs of dubious efficacy that were sold at unusually high prices. This was said to result from a combination of patent protection for new chemical formulas, consumer and physician ignorance, and weak incentives for physicians to minimize patient drug costs.[1] It was argued that drug companies devoted inordinate amounts of research to the development of patented new drugs which represented only a minor modification of existing formulas. The companies would then, it was said, exploit the patent protection by expensive promotion campaigns in which extravagant claims for the effectiveness of the new drug were impressed upon doctors and (sometimes) patients. Since most doctors were thought to lack the pharmacological expertise necessary to evaluate new drugs, it was believed that they relied heavily on information supplied by the drug companies. It was argued that they frequently treated this information with insufficient initial skepticism. Moreover, they seemingly would have little incentive for a careful evaluation of drug company claims since prescription costs were borne by their patients. It was said that some patients who might otherwise question the cost-effectiveness of drugs prescribed for them appeared to be entranced by accounts of the curative powers of new drugs, so that they frequently pressured the more skeptical doctors to prescribe these new drugs.

Even where patent protection was weak, as for new products that were combinations or duplicates of existing chemical formulas, it was argued that consumer ignorance and weak cost-minimization incentives made artificial product differentiation an attractive strategy. Since the patent laws provided some incentive to differentiation by chemical formula, physicians were faced with a mentally taxing array of complex chemical names from which to choose. It was said that this produced a reliance on easily remembered brand names, and that this, in turn, stimulated drug companies to concentrate on the production of easily remembered (and expensively promoted) brand names for old as well as new chemical formulas.

The Kefauver hearings characterized much drug innovation as socially wasteful. The waste was said to arise from product differentiation expenditures in an imperfectly competitive market permeated by physician ignorance: product differentiation expenditures were incorporated in prices which therefore did not reflect the "true value" of the drug to the consumer. It was argued that only in hindsight would doctors or patients discover that claims for new drugs were exaggerated: consumers would have been better off if they had used lower-priced old drugs (especially unpatented old drugs and most especially non-branded unpatented old drugs) instead of the new drugs. They would have paid less for treatment at least as effective as what they received. This view of the drug market was

7

summarized at the Kefauver hearings by a former drug company medical director:

> industry spokesmen would have us believe that all research is on wonder drugs or better medicinal products. They stress that there are many failures for each successful drug. This is true. . . . The problem arises out of the fact that they market so many of their failures. . . . Most [industries] must depend on selling only their successes. . . . [But] with a little luck, proper timing, and a good promotion program a bag of asafetida with a unique chemical side chain can be made to look like a wonder drug. The illusion may not last, but it frequently lasts long enough. By the time the doctor learns what the company knew at the beginning it has two new products to take the place of the old one.[2]

Senator Kefauver concluded that accurate information about new drugs would be provided only if the government regulated manufacturer claims of effectiveness. A proposal to institute such regulation was included in a bill he sponsored in 1961, and a modification of the proposal was incorporated in the 1962 amendments.

The 1962 Amendments

It is doubtful that the 1962 amendments would have been enacted without the thalidomide episode of 1961-62.[3] Thalidomide was, in fact, kept from the U.S. market by the FDA under provisions of the 1938 law. However, the manufacturer had distributed the drug to some physicians for experimental purposes. The 1938 law permitted distribution of this sort to those deemed by the manufacturer to be "qualified experts" as long as the drug bore a label warning the expert that it was still under investigation. The American manufacturer of thalidomide ended investigational distribution of the drug and withdrew its NDA after reports that deformed babies had been born to European mothers who had used the drug during pregnancy. These reports aroused concern that clinical testing of new drugs was insufficiently regulated. The lesson of the thalidomide episode appeared to be that, in the rush to market new drugs, producers were exposing humans to potential harm before that potential harm could be adequately evaluated.

The 1962 amendments to the 1938 Food, Drug and Cosmetic Act and the subsequent implementing regulations reflected both the concerns raised in the Kefauver hearings and those arising from the thalidomide episode. That is, they sought to change the conditions surrounding both the introduction of new drugs and their pre-market testing.

With respect to drug introductions, the amendments added a proof-of-efficacy requirement to the proof-of-safety requirement of the 1938 law, and they removed the time constraint on the FDA's disposition of a New Drug Application. No new drug may now be marketed unless and until the FDA determines that there is substantial evidence not only that the drug is safe, as required under the 1938 law, but that it is effective in its intended use. An effective drug, in this context, is one which the FDA determines will meet the claims made for it by the manufacturer. Promotion of the drug can claim no more than the effects established before the FDA, and must include a summary of "side effects, contraindications and effectiveness."

With respect to drug testing, the amendments and implementing regulations empower the FDA and the secretary of health, education and welfare to specify the testing procedure a manufacturer must use to produce acceptable information for evaluating his NDA. The manufacturer is now required, among other things, to submit a plan for investigations of the new drug (IND) in humans as well as information from pre-clinical testing. Periodic progress reports on the investigation are required. The FDA may terminate or order modification of the investigation at any point in the testing if the drug is deemed unsafe or ineffective.

If the 1962 amendments have been at all effective, they might be expected to have reduced the flow of new drugs marketed (if only by eliminating those deemed ineffective by the FDA but not by the manufacturer) and to have increased the gestation period for any new drug reaching the market. The latter effect would arise from the requirement for proof of efficacy, the removal of the time constraint on FDA action on the NDA, and the requirement for tests and evaluations that the manufacturer would not otherwise undertake. The added costs resulting from the expanded information requirements and delay of marketing would be expected to reinforce the reduction in the flow of new drugs.

The production of these effects would not necessarily tell us anything about the costs and benefits of the 1962 amendments. The costs and benefits would depend on the value of the particular drugs kept off the market by the amendments and the value of the information on new drugs generated by more extensive drug testing. A reading of the 1962 amendments can at best tell us the direction of change in drug innovation and its gestation period. It cannot tell us the magnitude of the change.

Before the costs and benefits of the amendments are examined, we want to know whether their effects on drug innovation have been substantial or small. If the amendments have kept few drugs off the market and caused little delay, their net benefits or costs might reasonably be ignored as trivial, unless they have at the same time substantially altered the average safety or efficacy of new drugs. Since the pre-1962 law gave the FDA the power to establish safety requirements, we would not expect the 1962 amendments to have altered the average safety of new drugs. To the extent that the FDA has required more extensive clinical testing of drugs to establish efficacy and has thus delayed drug innovations, however, safety may have benefitted by the greater opportunity to discover toxicity effects.

Plan of the Study

Chapter II attempts to establish the effect of the amendments on the flow of new drugs and their gestation period. These effects turn out to be substantial: the new drug flow is shown to be more than halved and the gestation period more than doubled by the amendments.

Chapter III outlines a method for measuring the net consumer benefit or cost of the amendments. The operating assumption is that the more effective a new drug, the more durable will be the demand for it—that is, the demand for ineffective drugs or drugs which do not live up to the claims made for them tends to decline in the light of cumulative physician-patient experience with them. On the basis of this assumption, economic theory is applied to provide a measure of the gains and losses yielded by any set of new drugs. For the sake of implementing this measure, the losses which arise from uninformed consumption of ineffective drugs are assumed to be eliminated by the amendments. While the same economic analysis is applicable to some aspects of drug safety, it is inadequate for unusually unsafe or unusually beneficial drugs.

The net benefits of the 1962 amendments are estimated in Chapter IV. These estimates indicate that consumer losses prior to 1962 were negligible. It follows, then, that little benefit has been produced by the amendments. It also follows that the severe decline in new drug flows produced by the amendments must result in a net loss to consumers. The loss is estimated at between $300 and $400 million annually as of 1970, or about 7 percent of total drug expenditures.

The evaluations of pre- and post-1962 new drugs by some "expert" groups are then examined to see whether these groups differ from ordinary consumers and the physicians prescribing for them in their judgment about the incidence of ineffective drugs. In general, the "experts" seem to agree with ordinary consumers (doctors and patients) that *there has been no substantial change in the efficacy of new drugs because of the amendments.* The conclusion that the decline in innovation has entailed a net loss to consumers is reinforced. An alternative measure of the loss resulting from ineffective new drugs is derived from one "expert" group's evaluations (the group being the AMA Council on Drugs): the estimate is that the loss amounts to at most 2 percent of total drug expenditures.

Finally, it is shown that the barrier to entry created by the amendments has resulted in slightly higher prices for old drugs. The annual cost to consumers from the barrier to entry is about 1 percent of total consumer drug expenditures. Chapter IV concludes that the 1962 amendments impose a net cost on consumers in excess of 5 percent of their drug expenditures.

Chapter V analyzes effects of the amendments on unusually harmful or beneficial new drugs. The analysis focuses on effects of these drugs on the earnings of those who use them and on costs of disease treatment. It is shown that a moderate increase in the gestation period for beneficial drugs costs far more than the savings from complete suppression of harmful drugs. This conclusion need not be modified even if it were assumed that a drug such as thalidomide would occasionally have been widely marketed in a pre-1962 environment, but would have been suppressed under the amendments (in fact, of course, thalidomide was suppressed in the pre-1962 environment). The specific costs and savings attributable to the amendments are uncertain. It is shown, however, that their potential cost is high. Had the amendments been passed a decade or two before 1962, the net cost of delayed marketing of new drugs would have been sufficient to double the total cost of the amendments as computed in Chapter IV—assuming that the drugs involved were not prevented from reaching the market eventually, that is, were not among those never developed because of the increased cost of meeting post-1962 FDA requirements. Similar potential costs are shown to be inherent in delay of innovations in health problems currently engaging pharmacological research.

While the 1962 amendments appear to have harmed their intended beneficiaries, the drug consumers, a complete accounting should include effects on the wealth of drug producers. These are estimated in Chapter VI, using drug company stock prices. The amendments appear to have had little net effect on the wealth of drug company owners, but appear to have reduced the riskiness of their investments. If owners are assumed to be risk averse, it may be concluded that they have benefitted from the amendments.

CHAPTER II

THE INTRODUCTION
OF NEW DRUGS

By virtually any measure, the rate of new drug introductions to the U.S. market has declined substantially since the passage of the 1962 amendments. The most important new drugs, both therapeutically and in development cost, are "new chemical entities" (NCEs).[1] These are drugs containing a single chemical formula not previously marketed. In the decade before the amendments, an average of forty-three NCEs was introduced annually compared with an annual average of sixteen in the subsequent decade.

The decline has been larger for other types of new drugs— combinations of previously introduced chemical entities and previously introduced chemical entities marketed under a new brand name (usually by a different manufacturer and sometimes for a different therapeutic indication). The pre-amendment decade saw an average of 301 new drugs of these types introduced annually compared with an average of ninety-two annually from 1963 through 1971.

Of course, simple comparisons of this sort cannot tell us how much of the decline can reasonably be attributed to the 1962 amendments. The possibility must be allowed for that the post-1962 decline in innovation might be the result of something other than the amendments. Indeed, one cannot rule out the possibility that the net impact of the amendments has been to stimulate innovation: if FDA pre-marketing certification of efficacy increased doctor confidence in the value of new drugs, manufacturers might find doctors more receptive to new products than they were formerly. This could increase the demand for new drugs and thus motivate manufacturers to develop more new drugs than they otherwise would have brought to market. It is therefore important to establish what rate of innovation could have been expected in the absence of the 1962 amendments.

Innovation and Market Growth

The economist who seeks to isolate the important determinants of the rate of innovation is confronted by the folklore view that innovation is essentially random or accidental. This is especially the case for research on drugs, where much is made of the serendipitous character of the innovation process. Many are familiar with the story of how Fleming discovered penicillin by observing the effects of a mold that accidentally contaminated one of his cultures. But economists are congenitally reluctant to believe that the outcome of any activity involving the use of scarce resources is purely random. Indeed, economists have met with some success in explaining the production of innovation within the ordinary framework of supply and demand. Schmookler, for example, was able to rationalize U.S. patent activity as a response to anticipated sales of the goods embodying innovations, with anticipations being largely determined by present sales of similar goods.[2] Put simply, he found that the supply of innovation is a response to the demand for innovation.

It appears that a process similar to that proposed by Schmookler can successfully rationalize pre-1962 drug innovation, and thereby shed light on the effects of the amendments. A formal model of the demand for drug innovation and its empirical counterpart is developed in the appendix. The essential results are summarized here.

Schnee reports that the bulk of pre-1962 introductions of new chemical entities took place within one to three years from the beginning of the development process.[3] If drug producers form expectations of future drug sales from present experience, this lag would suggest that present market conditions will affect innovations about two years hence. This kind of relationship may be seen clearly in Figure 1. The solid line shows the number of NCEs introduced each year. The dotted line shows the growth rate in the number of prescriptions billed two years earlier. There is a close correspondence between the two lines before 1962: the correlation coefficient is $+.75$. In particular it may be seen that there are two distinct cycles in NCE introductions (1948-1955 and 1955-1962). Both of these were foreshadowed by cycles in drug market growth.

The close correspondence between NCE introductions and drug market growth in 1959-1962 is especially important for interpreting post-1962 events. The FDA has sought to absolve the 1962 amendments of responsibility for the post-1962 decline in innovation by

Figure 1

NEW CHEMICAL ENTITIES, 1948-71

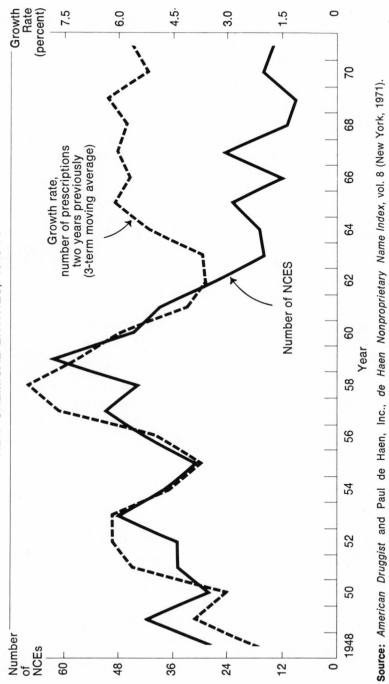

Source: *American Druggist* and Paul de Haen, Inc., *de Haen Nonproprietary Name Index*, vol. 8 (New York, 1971).

15

characterizing it as a simple continuation of a trend evident long before the amendments were enacted.[4] This explanation cannot be accepted. Figure 1 indicates that drug market growth increased in the years just before 1962: this should have produced a subsequent reversal of the 1959-1962 decline in NCEs. No such reversal occurred. Indeed the peak post-1962 innovation rate does not exceed the low 1962 rate.

There may be observed, especially after 1963, a persistently wide gap between the solid and dotted lines in Figure 1. To be sure, drug market growth never regained its mid-1950s peak. We might not therefore expect post-1962 NCE flows to have matched their pre-1962 peak. However, the average post-1962 lagged drug market growth rate (5.5 percent) is in fact slightly higher than its pre-1962 counterpart (5.1 percent). On this account we would have expected an average post-1962 NCE flow at least as great as the flow before 1962. The conclusion would seem to be that the 1962 amendments have been responsible for substantially *all* the post-1962 decline in drug innovation.

If there are feedbacks from innovation to market growth—if, for example, some of the substantial increase in market growth in the mid-1950s could be attributed to the preceding increase in innovation—this conclusion is strengthened. A feedback of this sort would mean that the amendments reduced the height of the dotted line in Figure 1 for the most recent years. This would cause us to underestimate the innovation rate to be expected in their absence.

Evidence supporting the dominant role of the amendments in the post-1962 decline in innovation is provided in Wardell's comparison of U.S. and British NCE flows.[5] He shows that for 1960-61, the U.S. NCE flow was 1.13 times the British, while for 1966-71 the U.S. to British NCE ratio was only .52, or 46 percent of the pre-1962 value. This last figure is roughly comparable to (though higher than) the ratio of 1966-71 U.S. NCEs to the number expected on the basis of drug market growth (.34).

It is likely that recent British NCE flows also are retarded by the working of U.S. law. Most British NCEs are produced by firms with substantial U.S. sales, which means that the British NCE flow is reduced whenever the cost of complying with the U.S. law deters development of an NCE for both markets. While it is not possible to determine how many more British NCEs there would have been in the absence of the amendments, the simple comparison of British and U.S. NCE flows surely does not exaggerate the effect of the amendments in the U.S. It corroborates the size of the effects shown by comparing actual NCE introductions with the NCE introductions that could have been expected on the basis of post-1962 growth of the drug market.

Sales of New Drugs

These effects might be mitigated if sales per new drug increased. The increase would occur if purchasers were more confident of the value of new drugs now than they were before FDA certification of efficacy. In addition, if some of the costs of complying with the amendments were fixed—that is, if they were unrelated to the size of a new drug's market—manufacturers might seek to amortize these costs by introducing drugs with higher expected sales volumes. There is, however, no strong evidence that drug manufacturers have achieved larger output per NCE since 1962 than they did before 1962, although there is evidence presented below that they have tried to do so.

Using a sample consisting of "important" NCEs (that is, NCEs which account for 1 percent or more of prescriptions sold in a submarket which itself accounts for over 1 million prescriptions annually), we find that the percentage of all drug prescriptions accounted for by these important NCEs one year after introduction fell from 1.58 in the period just before the amendments (1960-62) to 0.57 subsequently (1964-69, with the transition year 1963 excluded). This decline roughly parallels that in the number of NCEs introduced. Each NCE captures about the same share (one-tenth of 1 percent) of total prescriptions in each period.[6]

Since 1962 manufacturers have, perhaps in response to the high fixed costs of complying with the amendments, concentrated innovation on larger submarkets. Specifically, the average submarket penetrated by one or more important NCEs in a post-1962 year accounted for 3.49 percent of all drug prescriptions compared with a figure of 1.82 percent before 1962. This difference is statistically significant. An explanation for the failure of manufacturers to achieve higher sales per NCE in spite of their concentration on large markets is provided in the analysis of Chapter III.

Length of the New-Drug Development Process

The evidence available suggests that the proof-of-efficacy and clinical-testing requirements of the 1962 amendments have added at least two years to the gestation period for new drugs. The FDA reports that the average time between filing and approval of a

New Drug Application was seven months in 1962.[7] This rose steadily to thirty months by 1967, and has averaged twenty-seven-and-a-half months for the period 1967-72.[8] These figures are roughly in the middle of the one-to-four year range estimated by one drug company research director.[9]

The amendments have also, of course, added to the information required before the NDA is filed. The same research director estimates that the average development time for each NCE is now fifty-one to 105 months. The midpoint of this range exceeds by about four years Schnee's estimate of two years for the same process before 1962. Even when generous allowance is made for considerable variation in drug development time, it is difficult to attribute less than two years added development time to the operation of the 1962 amendments.

This conclusion is supported by data in Wardell's study.[10] He has established the year of introduction in each country for each NCE introduced into both the U.S. and Britain for 1962-71. In the 1962-65 period, when the full effects of the amendments had not yet set in, the U.S. led Britain by an average of 6.6 months per drug introduced in both places. However, in 1966-71, Britain led the U.S. by an average of 15.3 months per drug. This change—almost two years—may be regarded as a minimum estimate of the extent to which the amendments currently delay introduction of new drugs.

CHAPTER III

COSTS AND BENEFITS OF THE 1962 AMENDMENTS: ANALYTICAL FRAMEWORK

Chapter II has shown that the 1962 amendments have reduced the annual flow of new drugs by about 60 percent, have reduced total new drug sales by a comparable amount, and have delayed by two years or more the marketing of those drugs which have been introduced. In short, the amendments have had a substantial quantitative impact on the market for new drugs. However, it remains to be shown whether this "drug lag" has, on balance, helped or hurt consumers and by how much, because some of the twenty-five or so additional NCEs that would otherwise have been introduced each year might have been inefficacious. This chapter outlines a procedure for estimating the gains and losses to consumers from the nonintroduction or delay of drugs, and thereby measures one effect of the 1962 amendments.

Use of Consumer Behavior

The procedure will focus largely on physician and consumer evaluation of drugs as observed in the marketplace. This choice of focus may be controversial. It deserves explanation. One could approach the problem by relying on the judgment of nonconsumer "experts" to determine which drugs were worthwhile and which were not. On this approach, if experts judge drug X to have no more medical effectiveness than aspirin, it might be concluded that consumers would benefit if X were not on the market, the benefit equalling the sales of X less the cost of a medically equivalent amount of aspirin. I largely eschew this approach, partly to maintain a sensible division of labor: an economist's expertise does not, after all, lie in resolving pharmacological disputes.

There is, however, a more fundamental problem that arises when expert judgment and consumer behavior differ persistently. Let us assume that before X is marketed all interested parties—drug manufacturers, the FDA, doctors and patients, and so on—agree unanimously on who is best qualified to evaluate the drug's pharmacological properties. Let us assume further that the disinterested expert finds that X and aspirin are indeed pharmacologically equivalent, and (what will be important for subsequent analysis) assume also that every interested party is informed of this finding. Now with this information in mind, let us assume that doctors persist in prescribing X and patients persist in buying it at a substantial premium over aspirin. In such a case, the doctors and patients would, given their own preference for X, suffer a loss rather than a benefit if X were not marketed. Exclusive reliance on expert judgment would then lead to inaccurate benefit-cost estimates, unless of course one wished to simply ignore benefits consumers receive from behavior that deviates from what is prescribed by the "experts."

I am aware that many readers may, implicitly or explicitly, wish to leave out of account benefits and costs resulting from what they may regard as irrational (even if fully informed) behavior. These readers are referred to a subsequent section in Chapter IV in which costs are imputed to the "irrational" behavior of informed consumers. Fortunately, the margin of error here is probably smaller than it would be, for example, in evaluating benefits and costs of policies designed to regulate smoking and diet patterns. In these cases, the behavior prescribed by experts and the behavior engaged in by informed consumers often differ markedly. There may also be drug consumers who will respond, somatically or psychologically, to an appropriately marketed placebo in more or less full knowledge of its chemical properties. But it would require strong assumptions that I am unwilling to make in order to believe that this group would be numerous. If most consumers are seeking improved health through their drug consumption, and if the effect of drugs on health can be predicted from their chemical properties, then most of those buying placebos will be both ignorant and unhealthy. If this group is not numerous, one can avoid choosing between contenders for the status of "expert" and rely instead on the behavior of informed consumers to evaluate the benefits and costs of drug consumption patterns. This, of course, requires specification of what constitutes an "informed" consumer.

While lack of information may be the most important source of difference between the behavior of doctors and patients in the marketplace and that which experts might prefer, one must not minimize the conceptual difference between the approach used here and one which relies completely on expert evaluation of drugs. I will use expert evaluations of drugs in this study to check the reasonableness of my conjecture on the empirical significance of this difference in the drug market.[1]

The Consumer Surplus Approach

The method used in this analysis relies on the venerable economic doctrine of "consumer surplus." Since some readers may be unfamiliar with this doctrine, a brief explanation is in order at this point.

The idea of consumer surplus derives from the basic postulate of economics that the lower the price of a good, the more any group of consumers will purchase. This inverse relationship between the price of a hypothetical good (measured vertically) and the amounts purchased by consumers (measured horizontally) is illustrated in Figure 2. In the example used, one unit would be purchased if the price were 20 cents. Each one cent price reduction would stimulate a one unit increase in consumption.

This behavioral relationship, or demand curve, also contains information about the value consumers attach to their use of the good in question. Perhaps the easiest way to understand this is to imagine that any individual consumer will purchase no more than a single unit no matter how low the price. In that case, the inverse price-quantity relationship holds true because more consumers are attracted to buy the good at lower prices. This assumption is made for purposes of this example only. It is more restrictive either than economic theory suggests or than the subsequent results require.

Consider, nevertheless, the situation when the price of the good is 20 cents. Only one consumer buys it. His willingness to part with 20 cents indicates that the good is at least this valuable to him. Since no one else purchases the good, we may conclude that the good is worth less than 20 cents to all other potential consumers. Now suppose the price falls to 19 cents. A second consumer buys it and thus reveals to us the worth of the good to him: at least 19 cents but no more than 20 cents. We also know that our first consumer now receives a net benefit, or "consumer surplus," of at least 1 cent: he pays 19 cents for a good whose worth to him is at least 20 cents.

By similar reasoning, if the price fell to 18 cents, we could deduce the total net benefit to all three consumers who would then purchase the good: this would be at least 3 cents—at least 2 cents

21

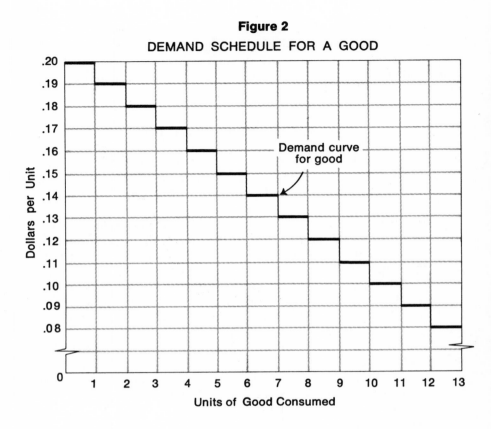

Figure 2

DEMAND SCHEDULE FOR A GOOD

Demand curve for good

Dollars per Unit

Units of Good Consumed

to the first consumer, 1 cent to the second and nothing (or at least less than a cent) to the third. The consumers, treated as a group, achieve this net benefit because they part with 54 cents (three units at 18 cents per unit) for goods worth at least 57 cents (20 + 19 + 18 cents) to them. This example illustrates how one may quantify the common sense notion that the lower the price consumers pay for a good, the better off they will be.

Geometrically, what is involved here is the calculation first of the area beneath the demand curve—the sum of the varying heights (in this case 20, 19 and 18 cents)—and then the deduction from this total value of the expenditures required for the goods purchased. The reader may, by applying the logic of the consumer surplus theory just given, determine that if the price of the goods were as low as 10 cents consumers would receive a total net benefit of at least 55 cents on the eleven units purchased. To arrive at this figure, he would deduct total expenditures on the eleven units at the 10 cent price ($1.10) from the total area underlying the demand curve up to eleven units ($1.65, or 20 + 19 + 18 + ... + 10 cents).

The example given assumes implicitly that the consumer knows the value of a good to him when he buys it, or that any guess he makes (or any advice via prescription by his physician) is correct. But the 1962 amendments contemplate the quite different possibility that a consumer may willingly pay a given amount for a good (a drug) prescribed by his physician because of exaggerated advertising claims, but that the true worth of the drug to him may fall short of this amount. If that true worth is, say, 5 cents, and the expected value is 20 cents, then far from receiving a net benefit of 2 cents with the price at 18 cents, he will suffer a 13-cent loss. We wish to incorporate this possibility into our analysis.

One way to do this, for a group of consumers, is to examine behavior at different points in time. If physicians persistently believe exaggerated claims of new drug efficacy, we should observe a heavy demand for new drugs immediately after the bulk of doctors have been exposed to the claims, and then a decline in demand. If the efficacy claims were in fact exaggerated, we would expect some physicians to learn this from their own practice, from that of colleagues, from the medical literature, and so on. Unless the majority of physicians were perverse, we would expect that this learning process would, over time, erode the demand for the new drug. Put differently, the quantities doctors would be willing to prescribe would be revised downward. Once this learning process is complete, a comparison of the resulting demand with the initially overoptimistic demand can be used to measure the gross loss from exaggerated efficacy claims.

The method by which this gross loss can be measured is illustrated in Figure 3. (For ease of exposition, demand curves are drawn as continuous rather than as stepped functions.) Suppose a new drug, X, is marketed at a price OB, and that the consumers' initial evaluations of X lead them to have the demand curve illustrated by the line ADM. In that case, OC units will be bought initially for OBDC (= OB × OC) dollars. The net benefit consumers expect these OC units to provide is the area BDA (the gross benefit, OADC, less expenditures, OBDC).

Now let us suppose that physicians discover that X is not as valuable as they originally thought, that the manufacturer has overstated what they discover to be the drug's effects. At this point the value placed on the drug is reduced, and the demand curve falls to GHEN. Consumers now buy only OF units, and the genuine net benefits these provide are BHG dollars per unit time. Consumers

Figure 3
DRUG DEMAND CURVES

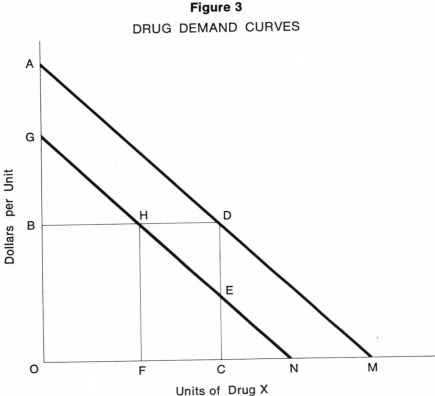

also discover that they have wasted money. Before the true merits of the drug were discovered, extra FC units of the drug were bought. The true gross value of these was HECF, but HDCF dollars were paid for them. These extra FC units therefore entailed a net loss of HDE dollars for the time it took to learn the drug's true value. In the extreme, where consumers discover the drug to be totally worthless, demand for it would become nil (none would be bought at any price), and the losses would be the total initial expenditure, OBDC.

In the context of this analysis, the rationale for the 1962 amendments would be that, by relying on the expertise of the FDA, physicians would not prescribe inaccurately and consumers could avoid losses such as HDE or OBDC. That is, the FDA would screen manufacturer efficacy claims and prevent physicians from being confronted by those claims which would have caused them to prescribe the extra FC units. In this way, both the initial and subsequent demand for X would be GHEN. The costly learning process would be avoided. One must remember that consumers might have to pay something for this information since the costs of the added testing required of drug manufacturers might be reflected in a price above OB. This higher price would cause net benefits to be less than BHG per unit time. One must also remember that, in practice, the 1962 amendments entail delay in marketing new drugs. Consumers will lose benefits (BHG) during the entire period of the delay. But so long as the value of these lost benefits falls short of the prospective losses (HDE) the 1962 amendments would yield consumers a net gain.

This analysis raises important problems if we try to generalize its view of the incompletely informed physician in the pre-1962 environment. What physicians learn about some new drugs from their experience should affect their evaluation of other new drugs. If, for example, they find that they consistently overestimate the benefits of a particular manufacturer's new drugs, they will discount his claims about future new drugs and the initial and "true" demand curves will come together. *But we must minimize the empirical importance of this more general learning-from-experience process if we wish to entertain the possibility that the 1962 amendments have conferred net benefits on consumers.* Similarly, we must assume that, before 1962, there were few private sources of information which would quickly reduce the difference between ADM and GHEN. For the purposes of my analysis, I shall assume that in the pre-1962 drug market such differences may have been numerous and persistent. I will also treat the pre- and post-1962 drug markets as mutually exclusive and exhaustive states of the world.

One problem in the empirical implementation of this analysis is that a controlled experiment, one in which the same consumers buy the same drug with the same physicians advising them under two different regulatory environments, is not possible. As a practical matter, we can only compare the behavior of demand for new drugs introduced before 1962 with that for new drugs introduced after 1962. If the amendments have produced net benefits, we ought to see a demand curve for post-1962 new drugs which is initially lower than for comparable pre-1962 new drugs. However, the demand for pre-1962 new drugs ought to decline over time while that for post-1962 new drugs does not. Or, since the demand for new drugs could of course change over time for reasons unconnected to the regulatory environment, we would at least expect to see the pre-1962 demand growing less (declining more) than the post-1962 demand.

There is, of course, the possibility that the amendments have generated net costs, rather than benefits, for consumers. This possibility arises from the restrictions on information supplied by drug producers. Manufacturers may no longer advertise effects other than those certified by the FDA in its approval of the New Drug Application. To the extent that a manufacturer is unable to demonstrate worthwhile effects to the satisfaction of the FDA, or (perhaps more likely) to the extent that he is unwilling to risk the costs of doing so, the demand for new drugs may be artificially restricted by the amendments. In the absence of advertisement of these effects, some consumers who could have benefitted from the new drug will not be advised by their doctor to purchase it. The restriction on advertising will not, of course, prevent all consumption of new drugs for nonsanctioned purposes. However, it will raise the cost and presumably decrease the amount of privately produced information supplied with each new drug (including information which physicians and consumers would find valuable). It may be noted that prescription for nonsanctioned use only substitutes other costs, such as increased physician experimentation and greater exposure to malpractice suits, for the costs of explicit compliance with the amendments.

In addition to their direct effects, the amendments could well have had secondary effects in reducing the amount of information possessed by physicians about new drugs. Doctors cannot form an evaluation of products of whose existence they are ignorant. Some physicians will learn about a new type of drug when it is introduced to them as Brand A. If the potential seller, faced with the cost and uncertainty of complying with the amendments, never markets Brand A, the doctor may remain ignorant of the new drug type. He will therefore not seek out Brand B. In this way, the decision not to market A reduces information about the new drug type and the demand for it generally. More to the point, with neither Brand A nor Brand B on the market, physicians cannot express an evaluation of the drug type in any tangible way, so that demand for it will be nonexistent. It was shown previously that essentially all the drastic post-1962 decline in the number of new drugs can be attributed to the amendments. This source of reduced demand for new drugs may turn out to be more important than the explicit restrictions on promotion.

Previously we posed an extreme case in which we assumed the amendments provided benefits with no costs. To illustrate how the various restrictions on new-drug information contained in the amendments might impose net costs on consumers we may counterpose another extreme case in which they impose costs with no benefits. Figure 3 may again be used to illustrate this. Suppose that ADM is both the initial and true demand for a new drug (or group of new drugs) introduced before 1962, so that the true net benefits to pre-1962 consumers is the area ABD. Now suppose that an otherwise identical set of new drugs is marketed after 1962, but, because of the restricted information about them (including that arising from the failure of some members of the set to appear on the market), the demand manifested by post-1962 consumers is only GHEN. In this case, the net benefits of the new drugs are only GBH, and consumers are foregoing net benefits of GHDA (= ABD − GBH). These foregone benefits would measure the costs imposed by the amendments.

Let me recapitulate. I have distinguished two pure cases which provide a framework for measuring the net benefits or costs of the amendments. In the case where the amendments provide only benefits, the true demand for a set of new drugs will be like GHEN in Figure 3. Exaggerated effectiveness claims will, however, lead consumers to buy OC units initially instead of the OF units they will buy after physicians learn that the claims are exaggerated. The resulting net benefits of the drug to consumers are GBH minus HDE initially and GBH subsequently. The amendments, by eliminating only the exaggerated effectiveness claims, would cause the demand for the new drugs to be GHEN from the outset, and so eliminate the loss HDE that consumers would otherwise bear. The loss eliminated would measure the benefits from the amendments. In the case where the amendments impose only costs, the true demand for new drugs would be ADM, but the amendments restrict this to GHEN. This would result in missed benefits of GHDA. These would be the costs of the amendments to consumers.

The real world is of course more complex than these prototypes. For example, the true demand (without amendments) might lie below the initial demand (ADM) but above the post-amendment true demand (GHEN). In this case the amendments would provide some benefits and some costs. Alternatively, the benefits of the amendments could be supplemented by increased physician confidence in claims for new drugs which survive the FDA's scrutiny. The empirical manifestation of this would be post-amendments demand (and consumer benefits) in excess of the true demand without amendments. To measure the effects of the amendments on consumers I shall measure first the benefits provided by new drugs before 1962, net of the costs of learning what the benefits are, and then compare this to the net benefits derived from new drugs introduced after 1962. While it should be possible for the reader to interpret the empirical data in light of the discussion of the pure cases, these data will in fact be derived from a procedure that takes account of some important complexities. The procedure is summarized in a mathematical model presented in the appendix. The more important complexities treated in this model are as follows:

1. *Shifts in demand over time.* Since the true demand for new drugs can change over time, the benefits and costs of the amendments must be computed from the *relative* growth of this demand before and after 1962. Specifically, the demand should grow more rapidly after 1962 if the amendments yield benefits. This growth differential forms the basis for calculating the difference between initial and true demand, and consequently the benefits of the amendments. If growth of pre-1962 demand equals or exceeds that of post-1962 demand, it will be concluded only that the amendments have failed to eliminate losses like HDE in Figure 3, not that they have engendered similar losses of their own. That is, it is assumed from the outset that the amendments completely eliminate any exaggerated efficacy claims which would give rise to a costly learning process over time. Moreover, I rule out by assumption the possibility that any superior growth of post-1962 new-drug demand might be the result of slower diffusion of worthwhile information about the drug. (This might occur when a valid efficacy claim is not proposed or approved in the NDA process and cannot therefore be advertised to physicians.) These assumptions impart a conservative bias (a bias in favor of the amendments) to the empirical benefit-cost estimates.

2. *Present v. future benefits and costs.* It is a fundamental principle of economics that a dollar of benefit or cost incurred in the future is worth less than a dollar today. Consequently, whenever the relevant benefits or costs are spread over time, my estimate of their sum will be the present value of the future components of the stream.

3. *Drug prices.* The analysis assumes that the amendments have no effect on drug prices. For reasons given below, this may be unrealistic. Since the benefits or costs provided by the amendments depend on drug prices the empirical estimates allow for differences in prices among groups of new drugs.

To be more specific, the discussion has shown how the benefits and costs of the amendments can be deduced from shifts in the demand curve for new drugs. However, shifts in demand may induce sellers to change prices and so change benefits and costs. These demand-induced price changes would tend to increase the net consumer benefits (reduce the costs) of the amendments. If, for example, the seller charges OB when the demand curve is GHEN, a higher demand could lead sellers to charge more than OB. Therefore, even if ADM were the true demand curve, so that the amendments in fact imposed costs on consumers, it is the case that in the absence of the amendments the consumer would have received a net benefit less than ABD (because of the higher price with a higher demand) and his loss after their enactment would be less than AGHD. Similarly, if initial demand without amendments were inflated by exaggerated efficacy claims, it would engender a price above OB, and, therefore, the losses of learning from experience would exceed HDE.

The amendments have also affected the cost of developing and marketing new drugs, thereby rendering the overall impact of the amendments on new-drug prices ambiguous. The restriction on seller-provided information would by itself lower marketing costs and presumably lower prices. This would occur whether or not the extra information would have been "worthwhile." [2] However, the important proof-of-efficacy and clinical testing provisions of the amendments increase new-drug development costs. These provisions increase direct expenditures for research and development, increase the uncertainty of their payoff, and delay the payoff. These costs appear to be substantial: the amendments appear responsible for doubling the research and development costs of the average NCE.[3] Since these costs may raise prices, we cannot know *a priori* the net effect of the amendments on new-drug prices.

There is a similar ambiguity in the effects of the amendments on competition. The proof-of-efficacy requirements and the restrictions on drug advertising were designed in part to stimulate price rivalry. If the seller could not "artificially" differentiate his new product, the price he could get for it would be more sensitive to the prices of close substitutes. But there is another side of the coin. If the product never gets to the market, a source of new competition for existing sellers is removed. Since the amendments have proved an effective barrier to entry, there is at least the possibility that they have weakened rather than promoted price competition in the drug market. I shall therefore investigate the effects of the amendments on the prices and net consumer benefits of old as well as new drugs.

Drug Safety and Important Medical Advances

While I will rely on the procedure outlined for estimating and comparing the behavior of demand curves for new drugs, there are some cases in which it provides an inadequate measure of the costs and benefits of the 1962 amendments. Consider first the case of a drug which after being marketed is found to damage the health of some users far more than it improves the health of others. Even if the drug disappears from the market, the maximum loss to consumers implied by the procedure outlined will be consumer expenditures on the drug. This will clearly be an understatement since, apart from drug expenditures, consumers will suffer medical expenses, lost income, or even death.

If extended testing keeps a drug of this kind off the market by revealing its toxic effects before it is introduced, the analysis must be supplemented to arrive at a reasonable estimate of the benefits of the 1962 amendments. The requisite supplementary data are, however, too skimpy to permit more than an estimate of the order of magnitude of this benefit. The estimate may be found in Chapter V.

My procedure also hides important costs of the 1962 amendments for some drugs kept off the market or delayed in introduction. In considering effective drugs which the amendments keep off the market for some time, we want to know the maximum amount that consumers would have been willing to pay rather than go without the drug for that time. The procedure I have outlined gets at this by examining consumer reaction to drug prices: at higher new-drug prices, consumers substitute alternatives (old drugs, no drugs), and the more extensive this substitution, the less lost from new drugs not introduced. However, we can never directly observe consumer evaluation of a drug which is not marketed even if the consumer knows that such a drug exists.

In practice, these evaluations will be estimated by extrapolation from observable data: this will sometimes yield serious underestimates. An extreme example will clarify this. Suppose the drug whose demand is illustrated in Figure 2 is the only drug available that can cure an otherwise fatal malady for one of the consumers. Suppose in consequence, that this consumer would be willing to part with all his wealth of $1,000,000 rather than go without the drug. The highest price at which a single unit of the drug could be sold would therefore be $1,000,000 rather than the 20 cents shown, and the net benefit to all consumers from a price of 10 cents would be in the neighborhood of $1,000,000 rather than 55 cents. However, this information is unlikely to be provided by a demand curve derived from available data. For whatever reason—fear of competition or of government reaction or an inability to charge discriminatory prices—we will not observe a sale of the drug at a price anywhere near $1,000,000. Instead, the demand curve will likely reflect the response of consumers to prices which vary within the 10- to

20-cent range that establishes the basic market. In practice, the highest price that could be charged to any one consumer (or small group) will then be estimated by extrapolation from this normal market experience. Thus, the failure of drug sellers to collect this maximum price will result in a substantial underestimate of the losses entailed by keeping a drug with unusual therapeutic value off the market. Consequently, market data must be supplemented in order for us to estimate total losses. The method by which this can be accomplished is discussed in Chapter V.

Summary

The 1962 drug amendments sought to reduce the costs to consumers of ineffective drugs. To the extent that this goal has been attained, we would expect to see demand curves for new drugs which are higher or rising more rapidly after 1962 than the demand curves for new drugs before 1962. We would also expect to see these demand changes complemented by reduced new-drug prices resulting from reduced information expenditures by sellers or increased price rivalry among them. However, the benefits produced by the amendments have not been costless: some of the drugs and some of the information kept from the market would yield net benefits, unless regulators are omniscient and dealing with the regulators is costless. The costs in the form of foregone benefits will be manifested in a smaller difference in the level and rate of growth of pre- and post-1962 new-drug demand curves. Also, costs imposed by the amendments on new-drug producers and the reduced competition from new drugs facing sellers of old drugs would work to offset any reduction of drug prices. The primary object of the empirical work presented in this study is to establish the magnitude of the net effect of these different forces.

CHAPTER IV

ESTIMATED COSTS AND BENEFITS OF THE 1962 AMENDMENTS

This chapter uses the theoretical framework presented in Chapter III to estimate the net consumer benefits of the 1962 amendments. These estimates, derived from physician and consumer evaluations of new drugs in the marketplace, are then subjected to corroborative tests derived from the drug evaluations of "experts."

Consumer Evaluations in the Drug Market

Most of the data used in this section are taken from R. A. Gosselin, Inc., *National Prescription Audit* (NPA). Since they are hardly perfect for present purposes, some of their shortcomings must be mentioned. Output is measured by number of prescriptions sold and the corresponding price is average receipts per prescription. Moreover, the analysis does not focus on a single drug market, but the submarkets defined in the NPA ("therapeutic categories"). These are defined technologically by similarity of the chemical properties of the members. The potential inaccuracy in these data is substantial. The more expensive prescription may be the cheaper mode of therapy. Some drugs in one category may be closer substitutes for those in another than for those in the same category. While much of the potential inaccuracy must be accepted in order to use the data, I have attempted to reduce its probable magnitude in selecting the sample from the data.[1]

The sample is drawn from a period spanning the 1962 amendments. The amendments are presumed to have affected the markets for new drugs starting in 1964, and data on post-amendment new drugs are drawn from 1964-70. A sample of similar size is drawn from the three years 1960-62 just before the amendments. It may be noted that, since the innovation rate for these years was about 10 percent below the average of the pre-1962 decade, the resulting estimate of pre-1962 new-drug benefits and costs will be understated.

The primary use to which these data are put is the estimation of demand curves for new drugs. From these the net benefits to consumers of new drugs marketed before and after the amendments may be inferred. The way in which these demand and benefit estimates are obtained is described in the appendix. However, the basic rationale for these estimates can be understood by examining the data on new-drug prices and unit sales.

Table 1 presents some of these data. In order to standardize the new-drug prices and quantities for differing submarkets, the average price per new-drug prescription is measured against that of prescriptions for old drugs in the same therapeutic category, and unit sales of new-drug prescriptions against total category prescriptions. These figures are shown for the year following introduction of NCEs, since NCE market penetration tends on average to attain its peak within a year.

There are two salient characteristics of the data in Table 1. First, there is a substantial decline in the output of new drugs after

Table 1

AVERAGE MARKET SHARE AND RELATIVE PRICE FOR NCEs, IN YEAR AFTER INTRODUCTION

NCEs Introduced In:	Annual Average Number of Therapeutic Categories with NCEs (1)	Average Percentage of Category Prescriptions Which Are for NCEs (2)	Average Ratio of Price of NCEs to Price of Other Drugs in Category (3)
1956–57	11.0	13.2	1.223
1960–62	10.3	10.7	1.263
1964–69	5.4	6.4	1.165

Note: There are fifty therapeutic categories in the sample. Column (1) indicates the average annual number of these in which one or more important NCEs were introduced in the period indicated. Column (2) is the percentage of prescriptions in a category accounted for by important NCEs (in the year following their introduction), in categories where NCEs were marketed. Column (3) is average dollar value per NCE prescription divided by average dollar value of other prescriptions in category.

The 1956-57 category classification differs slightly from the later years and the coverage is less comprehensive.

Source: R. A. Gosselin, Inc., *National Prescription Audit.*

1962. For the typical post-1962 year both the number of categories penetrated by NCEs and the share they obtained in the markets penetrated were about half the pre-1962 average. Second, the surprising fact is that new-drug prices did not rise at the same time. I put the result this way, because the small decline in post-1962 new-drug prices shown in the table is not significant by conventional statistical criteria. Moreover, the fact that the 1956-57 and 1960-62 new-drug prices are roughly equal indicates that this failure of post-1962 new-drug prices to rise marks no departure from any long-term trend. Thus, the substantial increase in research and development cost which the amendments brought about was not translated into an increase in the price of new relative to old drugs.

The significance of these results for our purposes may be grasped by reference to Figures 2 and 3 and the accompanying discussion. In that framework, a decline in new-drug sales could have two *possible* sources or could come from a combination of the two. One possible source would be a rise in price while the demand curve remained unchanged. We can rule this out because, when adjusted for price changes of old drugs, new-drug prices did not rise. The remaining possibility is that the demand for new drugs has decreased (the demand curve has shifted leftward), so that fewer new drugs are purchased at the relative prices prevailing before 1962. In the terms of the previous analysis, the dominant source of the reduced post-1962 sales of new drugs is not that they became more expensive to consumers, but that the information restrictions resulting from the amendments (including the restriction on information resulting from a lack of new products being offered for sale) reduced the consumer demand for new drugs.

The question that must be addressed is whether this decline in demand reflects reduced consumer benefits or reduced losses. It may be recalled that one rationale for the amendments was precisely that the high pre-1962 demand in part reflected exaggerated claims of drug efficacy and that a more realistic appraisal of these claims would lower demand for new drugs and avoid wasted expenditure. On the other hand, if these exaggerated claims were relatively unimportant, the substantial decline in new-drug demand would imply a net reduction in the benefits consumers derive from new drugs. The analysis in Chapter III suggests that we can distinguish between these possibilities by examining the behavior of new-drug demand over time—that is, by observing whether or not the high pre-1962 demand tended to decline when efficacy claims could me matched against experience in the use of new drugs.

The measurement of the gains and losses from the amendments proceeds by stages. First, I treat the demand for new drugs initially observed in the market as if it accurately reflects the benefits derived from new drugs. Then I examine subsequent changes in new-drug demand to see whether, and by how much, the initial demand before 1962 in fact reflected inaccurate and overoptimistic estimates of new-drug benefits. Of course, when it is assumed that initial new-drug demand is accurate, the fact that the amendments induced a decline in demand translates into a net consumer loss from the amendments. That is, we would be computing the net benefits from the higher demand, deducting from those the lower demand and labeling the whole of the difference (an area such as GHDA in Figure 3) as a net loss. The procedure for arriving at this estimate, against which a deduction will have to be made subsequently for the reduced costs of learning resulting from the amendments, is detailed in the appendix.

The calculations show an estimated net cost to consumers of $42 million in the year following introduction of NCEs because of the decline in new-drug demand resulting from the amendments. Since NCEs remain on the market for many years, this decline in demand will persist over time and will result in losses after, as well as during, the first year of marketing. The total loss from restriction of drug innovation in any single year would be the present value of all future losses. If, for simplicity, the first-year loss is assumed to persist indefinitely, and future losses are discounted at the rate of 10 percent per annum, the present value would be $420 million. This is the value sacrificed each year that drug innovation is restricted.

It should be noted that the $420 million annual loss applies only to NCEs. No account is taken of the (perceived) benefits sacrificed because of lower rates of introduction of other new drugs. The reason for this omission has to do with the difficulty of accurately measuring the demand for combination products: it is given in detail in the appendix. To say that the demand for these drugs is difficult to measure does not, of course, imply that consumers think they have no net benefits. However, rather than resort to an arbitrary benefit estimate, I have chosen the most conservative procedure and imputed net benefits to NCEs only.

To estimate the extent to which the annual benefit loss of $420 million is exaggerated by inaccurate perception of the true worth of pre-1962 new drugs, we must look at the behavior of new-drug demand over time. If the amendments have dealt effectively with what once was an important problem, we should see the difference between pre- and post-amendment new-drug demand narrowing over time. Some relevant data are presented in Table 2, which shows new-drug prices and market shares both immediately and four years after initial marketing. It is assumed that four years of experience with a new drug is sufficient to reveal its true value. While choice of this period may be arbitrary, it is in part forced by the data. A longer period would leave an unreliably small sample of post-1962 drug data.

The data reveal a remarkable stability in the demand for new drugs over time. What is most important here, they show no substantial difference in this respect between pre- and post-amendment new drugs. None of the intertemporal differences in NCE relative prices or market shares is large or significant by conventional statistical criteria. If pre-amendment efficacy claims were substantially exaggerated, it would be expected that pre-1962 new drugs would not hold their initial market share as well as post-1962 new drugs, or that they would do so only if their prices were reduced once the

Table 2

WEIGHTED AVERAGE MARKET SHARES AND RELATIVE PRICES FOR NEW DRUGS, ONE AND FOUR YEARS AFTER INTRODUCTION

Drugs and Subperiod	Market Share (percent)		Relative Price Ratio	
	One year after intro-duction	Four years after intro-duction	One year after intro-duction	Four years after intro-duction
NCEs introduced:				
1960–62	8.3	8.3	1.414	1.327
1964–69	3.9	—	1.209	—
1964–66	4.9	3.8	1.184	1.221
Other new drugs introduced:				
1960–62	6.4	7.7	1.133	1.130
1964–69	2.4	—	1.206	—
1964–66	2.5	2.3	1.231	1.192

Note: See note to Table 1 for explanation of "market share" and "relative price ratio." Data are averages for those categories where new drugs were introduced. Unlike the data in Table 1, these averages are weighted by category share of total drug prescriptions to take account of disparities in the size of drug submarkets.

Source: R. A. Gosselin, Inc., *National Prescription Audit.*

exaggeration was revealed by experience in use. But the stability of market share and price for pre-1962 new drugs suggests that experience with them did not generally cause doctors and consumers to regard their initial evaluations as exaggerated. The exaggeration implied by the data in Table 2 is so slight as to cause only a minor revision of the estimated net loss to consumers from the decline in drug innovation brought about by the amendments. The reader is again referred to the appendix for the details of this revision: its end product is a net annual loss of approximately $400 million in consumer benefits from new drugs, if one assumes that new drugs have an indefinitely long market life. The perhaps more realistic assumption of a fifteen-year average market life for new drugs yields a $330 million net annual loss to consumers imposed by the 1962 amendments [2] (see Appendix, Table A-2).

The reader is cautioned against taking these estimates literally. They are best treated as indicators of the relevant orders of magnitude. Looked at this way, they suggest that the magnitude of the problem which the amendments were designed to solve was small, or that little of the problem was solved by the kind of regulation they established. At the same time, the reduced flow of new drugs attributable to this regulation imposes net losses on consumers roughly equivalent to a 5 to 10 percent excise tax on the $5 billion (1970) sales of all prescription drugs.

This conclusion holds when data on new drugs other than NCEs are examined. Table 2 shows the same temporal stability in relative price and output for these drugs both pre- and post-1962 as existed for NCEs. As with NCEs, the data suggest that any saving on inefficacious drugs because of the amendments would not compensate for missed benefits from drugs kept from the market. Given our assumption that net missed benefits from new drugs not introduced (other than NCEs) are zero, these data should strengthen confidence that the estimated net loss from the amendments has not been exaggerated.

The conclusion that the 1962 amendments have taxed rather than benefitted drug consumers is sufficiently startling to require corroboration. So far I have relied on the consumers' (doctors and patients) own evaluations of drugs to measure benefits and costs: I will now examine evaluations by presumably more sophisticated "experts." The purpose here is not to develop an alternative "paternalist" measure of costs and benefits. The working assumption is that expertise entails the ability to discover the "true" consumer interest. Thus, if there are pervasive differences between expert and physician evaluations, and these differences are reduced by FDA supervention, some doubt will be cast on the magnitude of the net costs we have attributed to the amendments.

Expert Drug Evaluations

I will here examine the possibility that groups who know more about new drugs than the typical physician and patient show behavior consistent with a belief that the proportion of new drugs which is ineffective has been reduced by the amendments. Since the amendments have produced a substantial reduction in drug innovation, they might have left consumers worse off on balance even if they prevented marketing of all ineffective drugs. At the same time, unless the amendments have prevented substantially more waste than is implicit in ordinary consumer behavior, there would seem to be no room for revising the conclusion that they have imposed net costs on consumers. The main purpose here is to see just how much doubt can be cast on that conclusion by substituting expert evaluation of drug efficacy for evaluation by doctors and consumers. The expert evaluations examined are those of hospitals, panels employed by state public assistance agencies, and the American Medical Association's Council on Drugs.

Hospital Drug Purchases. Hospitals account for about one-quarter of the value of manufacturer drug shipments. In many cases their drug purchase decisions reflect the prescribing habits of the same physicians who prescribe for the out-of-hospital market. However, to take advantage of large-scale purchase economies, many larger hospitals limit the bulk of their inventory to a standardized drug list (formulary) developed by a specialized committee. Doctors are encouraged or required to prescribe from the formulary.[3] There is enough difference in the putative sophistication underlying hospital and non-hospital drug purchase decisions to make a comparison between them useful. To be sure, that difference might be larger in hospitals affiliated with teaching or research programs than it would be generally, but comprehensive data are available only for all hospitals. The data are dollar sales of drugs to hospitals, with the drugs classified in the same therapeutic categories used for the out-of-hospital market.

If hospital purchasers were able to discern ineffective drugs better than less sophisticated and overoptimistic ordinary buyers before the ordinary buyers had the aid of the amendments, we should see the following:

(1) Prior to 1962, new drugs should have taken a substantially greater share of the non-hospital than of the hospital market, because hospitals would ignore some efficacy claims that impressed ordinary buyers.

(2) After 1962, this difference in market shares should narrow or disappear, because the FDA, in screening efficacy claims, would be providing the ordinary physician with the same kind of expertise enjoyed by the hospitals.

(3) The pre- and post-1962 new-drug shares of the hospital market should be the same, if the amendments do not keep effective drugs from the market.

A glance at columns (1) and (2) of Table 3 shows that all three expectations are amply fulfilled. The pre-1962 new drugs had a share of the non-hospital market more than twice as great as their share of the hospital market (column [1]). The difference was substantially eliminated for post-1962 drugs (column [2]). There is little difference between pre- and post-1962 hospital market shares (line 1, columns [1] and [2]).

Before these data are accepted as conclusive support for the hypothesis of a significant amendment-induced decline in the introduction of inefficacious drugs, one must examine the implications of consumer learning by experience. If the effective drug sold in the pre-1962 non-hospital market commanded no more than the 4 to 6 percent share characteristic of the hospital market in both periods

Table 3

WEIGHTED AVERAGE PERCENTAGE OF THERAPEUTIC CATEGORY SALES ACCOUNTED FOR BY NCEs ONE AND FOUR YEARS AFTER INTRODUCTION

Market	One Year After Introduction		Four Years After Introduction	
	Pre–1962 (1)	Post–1962 (2)	Pre–1962 (3)	Post–1962 (4)
Hospital	5.59%	4.87%	11.78%	6.47%
Out-of-hospital	14.02	4.67	13.60	4.14

Note: Sample comprises NCEs with sales to both markets (a few NCEs are sold only in one market).

Columns (1) and (3) employ NCEs introduced 1960–62, column (2) those introduced 1964–69, and column (4) those introduced 1964–67.

Source: Out-of-hospital data: R. A. Gosselin, Inc., *National Prescription Audit;* hospital data: R. A. Gosselin, Inc., *National Hospital Audit,* various issues.

(and of the non-hospital market after 1962), then we would expect (1) that the non-hospital market share would gravitate toward this figure over time as physicians learn from experience, and (2) that the hospital market share would remain stable over time because the initial judgments by hospital buyers are accurate. The data in columns (3) and (4) of Table 3, however, reveal a startlingly different pattern. It is the hospitals rather than the ordinary buyers who are the "slow learners."

With the passage of time, pre-1962 NCEs maintained their share of the non-hospital market, but fully doubled their share of the hospital market. The net result is that, after four years, hospitals were just as enthusiastic buyers of pre-1962 NCEs as ordinary buyers had been all along (the column (3) difference in market shares is statistically insignificant). In spite of a small increase over time in the hospital market share of post-1962 NCEs, hospitals ultimately find themselves about as restricted by the amendments as are ordinary buyers: without the amendments, they would apparently buy about twice as many NCEs as they do with them (columns [3] and [4]).

These remarkable results are difficult to understand. Perhaps they reflect risk aversion by large institutions where one wrong decision will inevitably affect many patients and be widely publicized. Perhaps they reflect only the slowness of committee decision making. In any case, they provide no support for the hypothesis that the 1962 amendments have kept a higher proportion of ineffective than effective drugs from the market. Indeed, an intriguing aspect of the Table 3 data is the *close agreement between the permanent effect of the amendments and the temporary effects of overcautious hospital purchases.* In both cases, half the effective newdrug sales are kept from the relevant market.

State Public Assistance Program Formularies. In recent years there has been a substantial increase in sales of prescription drugs financed from public funds. Under various state and local general public assistance and medical assistance programs, pharmacies are reimbursed for prescriptions provided at no charge or small charge to the clients of these programs. In an effort to control drug expenditures, several states have established formularies listing drugs eligible for reimbursement. Reimbursement for drugs not in the formulary is allowed only in unusual circumstances (emergencies) or requires extra effort by the physician.

While the methods by which these formularies are compiled vary considerably, some of the larger states delegate the task to specialized committees employing consultants with pharmacological expertise. Two formularies so compiled, those of California and Illinois, will be used here. Their general intent is to provide a list of least cost effective remedies for the range of symptoms likely to be encountered by prescribers. As such, they might be expected to screen out Senator Kefauver's *bête noir,* the high-priced therapeutic equivalent to what is already on the market.

If many drugs introduced before the amendments are ineffective, but few of those introduced subsequently, drugs introduced before the amendments should have disproportionately sparse representation in the state formularies. That is, when drugs in the formularies are classified by date of introduction, the pre-amendment group should constitute a smaller fraction of all pre-amendment new drugs than the post-amendment drugs included constitute of all post-amendment new drugs, other things being equal. (It may be noted that many drugs in either period will not appear in a formulary because they treat uncommon conditions.) The data in Table 4 do not, however, support this hypothesis. In the case of Illinois, the likelihood that a pre-1962 NCE and a post-1962 NCE will appear in the formulary is roughly equal. However, a pre-1962 NCE is in fact substantially more likely to appear in the California formulary than a post-1962 NCE.

To check the possibility that the "poor" showing of post-amendment NCEs might be attributable to bureaucratic inertia

Table 4

NCEs CLASSIFIED BY DATE OF INTRODUCTION AND APPEARANCE IN STATE FORMULARIES OF CALIFORNIA AND ILLINOIS

Date of Introduction	Number of NCEs in Formulary		Number of NCEs Introduced in Period	NCEs in Formulary as Percentage of NCEs Introduced	
	California (1)	Illinois (2)	(3)	California (4)	Illinois (5)
1946–62	221	158	516	42.8%	30.6%
1964–70	33	31	113	29.2	27.4

Note: Columns (4) and (5) are obtained by dividing columns (1) and (2) respectively by column (3) and multiplying by 100.

Source: NCEs by date of introduction: *de Haen Nonproprietary Name Index,* vol. 8 (New York: Paul de Haen, Inc., 1971); drugs in formularies: *Medi-Cal Formulary* (Sacramento: California Department of Health Care Services, 1971); *Drug Manual for Physicians* (Springfield: Illinois Department of Public Aid, 1971).

toward the newest NCEs, I calculated the percentages of 1964-67 NCEs appearing in both formularies. These percentages were virtually the same as those for the whole 1964-70 period. Thus the assertion by one expert group (the FDA) that post-1962 drugs are more effective than pre-1962 drugs is not corroborated by the action of another expert group (formulary committees).[4] The inability of independent expert groups to improve on the consistency of a random number table might imply that inefficacy is too difficult to define or that it is empirically trivial. Neither circumstance would be conducive to a major reduction in the incidence of inefficacious drugs, and the data in Table 4 are in fact inconsistent with any such reduction.

American Medical Association, Council on Drugs, Drug Evaluations. Since 1905 the AMA has conducted evaluations of drugs for its membership. Today this AMA evaluation is the largest such program outside government. The evaluations published in *AMA Drug Evaluations* summarize the existing pharmacological literature on each drug reviewed and make some judgment about the likely effectiveness of the drug. I attempted to extract from these drug evaluations the longest list of drugs of questionable efficacy for NCEs introduced in 1960-62 and 1964-70.

Opinions were found in the evaluations for eighty of the 111 NCEs introduced in 1960-62 and ninety-four of the 113 introduced in 1964-70. Any time the evaluations suggested that a drug could be ineffective, it was classified into one of two groups, either (I) not effective or (II) no more effective than other drugs. Since the opinions were frequently guarded and qualified, this required some arbitrary judgments. There are relatively few drugs which are called "not effective" without qualification. In addition to these few, any drug for which clinical data had not yet established effectiveness or was inconclusive was placed in group I.

Group I as calculated is surely too large, inasmuch as the AMA is willing to recommend use of many of the drugs in the group for certain indications.[5] However, the bias is deliberate, since we want here to establish an upper limit to the incidence of inefficacy. A drug was placed in group II if a less expensive alternative seems to be available for any important indication.[6] This group is also too large, inasmuch as it too contains drugs which are effective in some indications. Table 5 summarizes the resulting classification. It shows that ineffective drugs appear more frequently among pre-1962 NCEs, although the margin of difference is small enough to give a careful statistician pause. However, the data are worth further

43

Table 5

AMA COUNCIL ON DRUGS EVALUATIONS OF NCEs
1960-62 AND 1964-70

AMA Evaluation	1960–62 NCEs		1964–70 NCEs	
	Number (1)	Percent of total (2)	Number (3)	Percent of total (4)
Not effective	8	10.0	2	2.1
As or less effective than other drugs	8	10.0	7	7.4
Effective	64	80.0	85	90.4
Total evaluated	80	100.0	94	100.0

Note: See text for derivation of "Not effective" and "As or less effective than other drugs."

Source: *AMA Drug Evaluations* (Chicago: American Medical Association, Council on Drugs, 1971).

investigation: we have not previously encountered any data so suggestive of an amendment-induced reduction of the incidence of inefficacy.

Because the data seem to be worth further study, I estimated the dollar value of the "waste" entailed by purchase of drugs in groups I and II in the year following their introduction. All group-I drugs were assumed to have no therapeutic value, so that all consumer expenditures on them are counted as pure waste. For those group-II drugs which were as effective as cheaper alternatives, waste was computed to be the difference in per-prescription price times the number of prescriptions of the group-II drugs purchased. Where a group-II drug was less effective than an alternative, I arbitrarily assumed that equal therapeutic value could have been obtained for the cost of half of a prescription for the alternative: the resulting waste per prescription was then multiplied by number of prescriptions.

The resulting average annual bill for waste, adjusted according to 1970 drug sales, was $17.3 million for pre-amendment NCEs and $3.4 million for post-amendment NCEs.[7] If one assumes that this waste continues perpetually and if one then discounts the resulting stream at 10 percent per year, the present value of waste on each year's NCEs is ten times the figures given. These present values may then be compared with the counterpart estimates of consumer surplus (see Appendix, Table A-2 and Chapter III). The result is that, on an exaggerated estimate, about one-third of new-drug benefits are eroded by waste. But, what is relevant for our purposes, *this fraction is roughly the same for pre- and post-amendment NCEs.*

Thus, while the amendments seem to have reduced waste, they did not (in spite of the suggestiveness of the data in Table 5) reduce its incidence. They have therefore left consumers with a net loss. Indeed, the amount of pre-1962 waste was sufficiently small for this last conclusion to have held even if waste were eliminated after 1962.[8]

Moreover, if consumers learn from experience, it would be unreasonable to suppose that even this small waste would continue unabated forever. Given the crudeness of the waste calculation, any derivative data should be treated cautiously. It is nevertheless interesting to find some agreement between pharmacological experts and the judgment of the market. The market share of the sixteen pre-amendment drugs in groups I and II declined an average of 12.9 percent per year from the first to the fourth year after introduction. Only four of the sixteen drugs showed increased market shares. Since their price (relative to old drugs) also declined (by an average of 2.4 percent per year), the market share performance implies a substantial decline in demand for ineffective drugs. The drug consumers' ignorance is less than invincible.[9]

The last result, as tentative as it must be, may provide a clue to our difficulty in finding much effect from the amendments on the incidence of inefficacious drugs. Simply put, the effective new drug will tend to be more profitable than the ineffective new drug. To be sure, the ineffective new drug takes an initial market share and sells at a price roughly equal to that of other new drugs.[10] *Effective drugs do not, however, experience the substantial and fairly prompt loss of market share experienced by ineffective drugs.* Therefore, all other things being equal, the likelihood that a seller can recapture his investment in a new drug will increase with its effectiveness. *The penalties imposed by the marketplace on sellers of ineffective drugs before 1962 seem to have been sufficient to have left little room for improvement by a regulatory agency.* The only important reduction of sales of inefficacious new drugs brought about by the amendments seems to have come as a by-product of their reduction of the flow of all new drugs. *None of the data we have examined,* whether obtained from the evaluations of ordinary consumers or those of experts, *would have been very much different if, instead of detailed regulation, an arbitrary marketing quota had been placed on new drugs after 1962.*

The conclusions to which this examination of expert drug evaluation seems to point are these:

1. Experts are not unanimously agreed that the fraction of new drugs which are ineffective has declined since 1962. Rather, their judgments imply that this fraction is about the same today as before 1962.

2. To the extent that the data permit measurement, the costs of inefficacy seem to be small. This is suggested by the similarity of new-drug market shares in sales to buyers of varying pharmacological expertise (hospital versus non-hospital). The suggestion is confirmed by a direct estimate of what (according to pharmacological experts) consumers are wasting on ineffective new drugs. This figure is consistently much less than half the consumers' surplus generated by new drugs.

3. These conclusions are similar to those implied by the previous analysis of the behavior of ordinary physicians and consumers, where we found a trivial decline in demand for new drugs as they aged and a trivial difference in the rate of decline between pre- and post-amendment new drugs.

4. The analysis of consumers behavior assumed a gradual learning process that tends to eliminate waste on inefficacious drugs. The market behavior of a sample of new drugs deemed ineffective by experts seems to confirm the validity of that assumption.

Their decrease in demand and the generally stable demand for new drugs renders the losses from inefficacious drugs trivial compared with the surplus generated by other new drugs.

Effect of Innovation on Prescription Drug Prices

Perhaps the most extreme interpretation of the rationale underlying the 1962 amendments would be that most if not all new drugs bring no therapeutic improvement over existing drugs. The bulk of the preceding data—on market shares and prices of new drugs over time, expert drug evaluations, and so on—belies this view, but for present purposes I will accept it. If the consumer "should," but does not, treat old and new drugs as identical, his presumed gain and loss from regulation of drug innovation will turn completely on the impact of regulation on the prices he pays for drugs. That is, if he pays $1.50 for a new drug rather than $1.00 for an equivalent old drug, he would be saved 50 cents if the new drug were never marketed.

This view might rationalize even the most arbitrary restriction of drug innovation, since we have seen that new drugs sell at a premium over old drugs in the same therapeutic class (see Tables 1 and 2). Simple arithmetic would therefore seem to indicate that by reducing drug innovation the amendments have saved money for consumers.

This arithmetic would, however, ignore the effects of competition between producers of new and old drugs. If the producers of old drugs face a loss of market because new substitutes become available, they may be expected to respond by reducing prices so that the new-drug price premium becomes unattractively large for some customers. Thus, even if the entire initial price premium for new drugs were regarded as a waste, the overall effect of reduced drug innovation on consumer drug costs is ambiguous. The removal of a source of competition for producers of established drugs may reduce price rivalry, and the reduction in price rivalry may offset any savings on high-priced new drugs.

I attempted to measure the extent to which the price competition engendered by innovation overcomes the price premium for new drugs by examining the relationship between innovation and the behavior of the average price of old and new drugs treated as a single group. This was done both for the entire drug market and for the separate therapeutic categories. The details of the relationships I derived are in the appendix; I will summarize the major results here.

If there is little price competition between new and old drugs, one would expect that (because of the new-drug price premium) the greater is the sale of new drugs, the more the average price of an aggregation of old and new drugs would increase. In fact, above-average market penetration by new drugs generally leads to below-average price increases for the relevant aggregate of old and new drugs. For these purposes, the more relevant aggregate would appear to be the therapeutic category rather than all drugs lumped together: it would be unrealistic to suppose that a new tranquilizer would put competitive pressure on, say, prices of antibiotics.

The data in the appendix indicate that, over a two-year period, *if NCEs with a potential market share of 10 percent are kept from the market, the average prescription price in a therapeutic category will increase about 1⅓ percent more than it would otherwise.* This is not a substantial effect, but that it occurs at all is surprising in view of the alleged weakness of price competition between new and old drugs and in view of the price premium for new drugs. In any case, given the extent to which marketing of new drugs has been restricted since 1962, it is possible to conclude that prescription prices have been rising about one-tenth of 1 percent faster each year than they would have in the absence of the amendments. This estimate suggests that the cost to drug consumers from the anticompetitive effect of restricted innovation is about $50 million annually, based on 1970 drug sales.

Summary

The 1962 drug amendments sought to reduce consumer waste on ineffective new drugs. While this goal appears to have been attained, the costs imposed on consumers in the process seem to have outweighed the benefits. The reason for this is that the benefits are largely a by-product of a reduction of consumer exposure to all types of new drugs. The *incidence* of ineffective new drugs does not appear to have been materially reduced. Even if it had been, the pre-1962 waste on ineffective new drugs that might now be prevented appears to have been too small to compensate for the benefits consumers have had to forgo because of reduced drug innovation. The largest estimate of this annual waste prevention, based on ungenerous interpretations of the drug evaluations by the AMA Council on Drugs and pessimistic assumptions about consumer behavior, is $100-$150 million: this must be reduced by more than half to take account of the loss of market share of ineffective drugs over time.

In the present context, the forgone benefits of innovation show up as a decline in the demand for (and consequently the consumer surplus generated by) new drugs. In Chapter II, it was shown that essentially all the post-1962 decline in drug innovation—a reduction of over 50 percent in the number and output of new drugs—can be attributed to the 1962 amendments. This, combined with the absence of any increase in the relative price of new to old drugs, suggests a lower demand for new drugs. In part, this decline in demand simply reflects the fact that consumers cannot manifest a demand for products which are not marketed. However, the explicit restrictions on seller promotion of new drugs in the amendments and the reduced number of sellers who are informing consumers about new drug types have also contributed to this decline in demand.

The bulk of the evidence indicates that the post-1962 decline in demand does not reflect a more realistic physician appraisal of the genuine worth of new drugs. The pre-1962 demand did not fall after doctors had time to learn the worth of new drugs from experience as it would have if they were initially overoptimistic. Since doctors did not act as if they regretted their initial evaluations of pre-amendment drugs, the lower post-1962 demand for new drugs resolves largely into reduced net benefits ($300-$400 million annually) to drug consumers from a reduced flow of new drugs and information about them (and an additional $50 million annual cost resulting from reduced price competition). This conclusion is verified by assessments of experts and sophisticated drug buyers. The probability that they will assess a new drug as being ineffective is about the same for the pre- and post-1962 sets of new drugs and any reduced losses from ineffective drugs post-1962 merely offset a part of the missed benefits.

Finally, one ought to mention the direct budgetary cost of implementing the amendments, although this is relatively trivial. Of the total 1970 FDA budget ($66 million) it is unlikely that more than $15 million is attributable to the requirements added by the amendments.[11]

CHAPTER V

THE VALUE OF DRUG SAFETY AND OF IMPORTANT THERAPEUTIC ADVANCES

I argued in Chapter III that empirical demand analysis of the type summarized in Chapter IV would take inadequate account of the costs of unsafe drugs or the benefits of unusually successful drugs. The victim of an unsafe drug loses more than his drug expenditure. The beneficiary of an unusually successful drug gains more than the cost of the most expensive drug. It will not be possible here to measure these extra gains and losses in any precise way, but I hope to convey some idea of the magnitude of the extra gains and losses produced by the 1962 amendments.

This will entail placing pecuniary values on lives saved and spent and on illness suffered and avoided. To say the least, there is no universal agreement on how this should be done, and the reader should not be misled by the seeming precision of specific numbers.[1] For example, I will identify the value of a death or illness avoided with the present worth of the added earnings thereby engendered. The earnings lost through death and illness are surely an important component of the total loss but are just as surely not all of it. They leave out of account losses such as the bereavement of relatives, the pain of illness, and the costs of nonpecuniary income missed (as with leisure activities forgone). At the same time, alternative methods of valuing life would make deductions from earnings.[2] Any conclusion ought to be regarded as risky if it cannot survive doubling or halving of the cost estimate on which it is based. In the last analysis, I cannot hope to surmount the controversy and inaccuracy necessarily attending any mode of valuing life: I will, therefore, wherever possible, provide physical counterparts to the economic costs and benefits.

The questions I address here are these: (1) Have the 1962 drug amendments improved drug safety enough to pay for the tax they have imposed on consumers? and (2) has any substantial additional tax been imposed by restricted or delayed introduction of unusually beneficial drugs?

Drug Safety

Information on drug toxicity is never complete; some information may be revealed only after widespread human use. The producer of a new drug must take this into account in determining the length of the research and development process. The longer the process, the more extensive the toxicity information that is revealed before human use, and the smaller the likely costs from law suits or damaged reputation. At the same time, extending the research and development process entails forgone receipts from marketing of the drug.

The 1962 amendments presume that the consumer costs and benefits of more extensive clinical testing of new drugs were inadequately reflected in the incentives to producers. More specifically, the amendments presume that drug producers bear so small a proportion of the consumer cost of an unusually harmful drug that unusually harmful drugs will be overproduced: the harm they engender would more than offset the benefits of early introduction of beneficial drugs. The amendments force producers to undertake more extensive clinical testing of all drugs than they would otherwise undertake in order to correct this presumed overproduction of thalidomide-type drugs. An estimate of the magnitude of the costs arising from unusually harmful drugs before the amendments is therefore relevant to any evaluation of the amendments. Since direct expenditures on these drugs are a trivial part of the costs, this estimate will focus on the measurable health effects of unusually harmful drugs.

Chloramphenicol. Thalidomide-type products do not appear to have been introduced frequently in the years before 1962. Systematic data on their health effects are extremely rare. I will therefore have to rely for concrete data on the one case where these are available, and where adverse health effects of the type that the amendments might reasonably have been expected to reduce were present.[3] The case is that of the drug chloramphenicol, marketed under the trade name Chloromycetin.

This antibiotic was introduced in 1949 and met with immediate market success. Within the next three years, however, the drug was implicated as a cause of a sometimes fatal blood disease, aplastic anemia. In 1952, the FDA temporarily halted sales of the drug. It permitted their resumption with the drug's indications limited to a few infections such as typhoid fever. It is reasonable to suppose that, had the 1962 amendments been law in 1949, the relationship between chloramphenicol and aplastic anemia would have been discovered before marketing. It may be less reasonable to suppose that all users of chloramphenicol who perished in ignorance of its relationship to aplastic anemia would have been spared by such a discovery. After a precipitous decline from 1952 to 1954, chloramphenicol sales—and aplastic anemia deaths—more than recovered their pre-1952 levels by 1960. Users of the drug, knowing the risks, found them outweighed by prospective benefits. This seems to imply that the initial market reaction to knowledge of chloramphenicol's adverse effects might have been smaller had the knowledge been conveyed in a less dramatic fashion than it was in 1952. I will, however, assume that had the amendments been in force in 1949, the death rate from aplastic anemia would have been at the nadir it attained after the 1952 disclosure of chloramphenicol's link to the disease. I will ignore any benefits sacrificed by the exaggerated decline in chloramphenicol use which permitted this low death rate.

In Table 6 these assumptions are employed to estimate the benefits that would be produced by the amendments were a drug exactly like chloramphenicol to be proposed for marketing today. The first column of Table 6 shows the U.S. death rate from aplastic anemia from 1949 (year one) to 1955, the post-chloramphenicol low. Let us assume that, with the information generated by the extended clinical testing required by the amendments, the higher pre-1955 death rates could have been avoided. That is to say, all of the difference between the 1955 and any pre-1955 death rate is assumed to be attributable to mistaken use of chloramphenicol. This difference, multiplied by the current population, gives an estimate in column (2) of the lives that would be saved if the chloramphenicol twin were proposed today. I next assume that each person saved would earn the U.S. average personal income for forty-five years, and discount this stream at 10 percent to get the money value of a life saved.[4] In column (3), the aggregate value of lives saved is again discounted to get the present worth of lives saved in each future year. The $22.3 million total is the present value of the added earnings produced by the 753 people spared from death by aplastic anemia.

Table 6

ESTIMATED BENEFITS FROM AMENDMENTS FOR CHLORAMPHENICOL-TYPE DRUG INTRODUCED IN 1970

Years After Intro- duction	Death Rate Without Amendments (per 100,000) (1)	Deaths Avoided With Amendments (2)	Present Value of Deaths Avoided ($ millions) (3)
1	.43	81	3.1
2	.40	20	.7
3	.44	102	3.3
4	.53	285	8.3
5	.49	204	5.4
6	.42	61	1.5
7	.39	0	0
Total		753	22.3

Note: Column (1) is the death rate for aplastic anemia in the U.S., 1949-55, as reported in the source article.

Column (2) is calculated as (column (1) — .39) x 10 x U.S. population in 1970 (203.7 million).

Column (3) is calculated as $38,565 x column (2) discounted to year 1 at 10 percent. $38,565 is the present worth of 45 years of 1970 U.S. average personal income, $3,910, discounted at 10 percent.

Source: K. Smick, P. Condit, R. Proctor and V. Sutcher, "Fatal Aplastic Anemia: An Epidemiological Study of its Relationship to the Drug Chloramphenicol," *Journal of Chronic Disease,* vol. 17, 1964.

The conclusions that may be drawn from the chloramphenicol experience are not substantially modified by doubling or trebling the estimated saving. The anecdotal evidence nowhere suggests that drugs with the unknown lethal side effects of the magnitude of chloramphenicol were being introduced regularly before 1962.[5] Indeed, the magnitude of the chloramphenicol side effects appears unique for the U.S. drug market. Therefore, it would exaggerate their effectiveness to attribute to the 1962 amendments savings much in excess of those given in Table 6 as often as once or twice each decade. The annual saving of something on the order of 100 lives is surely an impressive achievement standing alone, but this saving must be placed in context. Its monetary value is only a small fraction of the loss otherwise imposed by the amendments. Adding the amendments' prospective benefits in improved drug safety to the benefits from reduced waste on ineffective drugs does not give anything approaching the sum of the costs the amendments have imposed by forcing consumers to forego benefits from effective new drugs. It would require an extremely large valuation of the nonquantifiable benefits of reduced mortality—say, several million dollars per life saved—for the amendments to appear as a break-even proposition.

Thalidomide. This point may be illuminated further by examining experience with thalidomide, the drug that motivated the amendments. For these purposes, I shall suppose that the U.S. failed to escape the thalidomide tragedy in 1961. While this supposition is contrary to what actually happened, it is made in recognition of the fact that the framers of the amendments could not have regarded the foreign experience with thalidomide as unique and unthinkable or unavoidable in the United States. Instead, the amendments reflect a presumption that it was the American "near miss" that was unique, and that something similar to the foreign thalidomide experience was bound to occur in the United States unless the amendments were adopted. This presumption—which implies that it is worth delaying the introduction of all new drugs to weed out the occasional thalidomides—is difficult to sustain even when the implications of the foreign experience for the U.S. are pessimistically drawn.

Thalidomide was marketed first and most extensively in West Germany and then in most industrialized countries outside North America. The incidence of the birth malformation induced by the drug was on the order of ten times greater in West Germany than elsewhere.[6] Had the thalidomide tragedy spread to the U.S., it would be reasonable to expect this to have been characterized by the lower incidence. However, since we are dealing with the type of conjectural tragedy that may have influenced Congress, it may be useful to extrapolate the unusual West German experience to the U.S. The total West German incidence of birth malformation from thalidomide was about four per 1,000 live 1961 births. Given the 1961 U.S. live birth rate and the 1970 U.S. population, this would translate into about 19,000 cases (compared to the 4,000 West German and more than 7,000 worldwide cases attributable to thalidomide).

It is, of course, difficult to measure the cost of something like these birth defects. But even if one is willing to treat the defects as the equivalent of death, the quantifiable savings of avoiding a thalidomide tragedy still do not offset the cost of the amendments. This can be seen if we make the extreme assumption that the birth defects are inconsistent with any productivity.[7] In that case the malady can for present purposes be equated with death, in which case the total cost of a thalidomide tragedy in the U.S. would be about $150 million.[8] Since the value of lifetime earnings for infants is much lower than for most adults (because of the longer time before any earnings are produced), this straightforward application of previous methodology might not be useful here. Another way of looking at the case is to ignore completely the utility of the victim's consumption and treat him solely as a burden on society. This would imply that (assuming zero lifetime productivity) we should take the discounted value of the victim's future consumption as the social cost. For 1970 U.S. per capita consumption, this cost would amount to about $550 million. Even if we assumed that (a) a thalidomide tragedy and a chloramphenicol tragedy would each occur once per decade without the amendments and that (b) chances for both are completely eradicated by the amendments, the quantifiable benefits would be well under $100 million annually. This is only a fraction of the quantifiable costs of the amendments.

Delay in Important Innovations

One could conclude from this discussion that the amendments' benefits are worth their costs if one assigns a suitably high value to the nonquantifiable costs of illness and death and makes suitably optimistic assumptions about the amendments' ability to reduce these. This procedure would be biased: just as the amendments have the potential for reducing death and disease, so they have the potential for increasing them, and this potential must be taken into account.

The potential comes from the longer gestation period for new drugs entailed by the amendments. Just as the costs of unsafe drugs are inadequately measured in Chapter IV, so are the costs of the longer gestation period for some beneficial drugs inadequately measured there.[9] These drugs are those for which even an exceptionally high price would leave the consumer with net benefits if the drug were available, but which are temporarily or permanently unavailable because the NDA has not been given approval, or because the manufacturer does not believe he can appropriate the benefits to a sufficient extent to make pursuit of the NDA worthwhile. The data underlying the analysis in Chapter IV (which are developed in the appendix) imply that the net benefits of the typical new drug would be nil if its price were about twice that of related old drugs. Clearly, new drugs which can prevent death or materially reduce disability would yield net benefits even at prices many times the prices obtaining for virtually any existing drug. The previous analysis therefore cannot adequately reflect the benefits lost when these new drugs are unavailable.

There are at least two problems in estimating the size of these lost benefits: identifying the specific effect of the amendments and quantifying the benefits forgone. The second problem may be illustrated by using aspirin as an example. Substantial delay of this innovation would likely have denied consumers benefits many times the cost of the drug. Most of these benefits would, however, have consisted of increased comfort rather than of any easily measured increase in productivity. As a practical matter, I will limit this investigation to drugs with measurable productivity effects—that is, drugs which can be directly related to reduced morbidity, mortality, or treatment costs. It should be understood that these are not the only drugs that can provide unusual benefits.

Establishing the link between important innovations and the amendments poses more formidable problems. Since 1962, there has been no innovation in the U.S. remotely comparable to penicillin or the sulfonamides in its effects on morbidity or mortality. But this is also true of countries with regulatory systems comparable to that of the U.S. before 1962. It would be dangerous to conclude from either fact that the costs of the amendments have been enormous or that they have been trivial.

The United States accounts for over a third of world drug sales and research and development expenditures. It would be implausible to expect that reduced innovation in this large market would not affect the world innovation total even over a period as short as a decade. But it would also be implausible to attribute the complete absence of penicillin-type advances anywhere to constraints on U.S. innovation.

In view of the difficulty in establishing the precise effect of the amendments on major drug innovation in the past decade, I have made the conservative assumption that there has been no effect. This means that any estimates of unusual benefits forgone are unavoidably conjectural. I have also assumed that no major innovation will be permanently kept from the market by the amendments (even though this may be overly optimistic) and that the amendments do not sufficiently inhibit the research process to delay discovery of an innovation's basic chemical properties. Unusual benefits will then be lost only during the extra time it takes to satisfy the testing and proof-of-efficacy requirements before marketing. The data in Chapter II suggests that this time is at least two years. While this is already a conservative estimate of the effect of the amendments, the delay might be shorter still for highly beneficial innovations: but this conjecture cannot be tested with available data. The analysis then focuses on the question, how much benefit would be lost if a major therapeutic advance came on the market two years later than otherwise? The data will permit the reader to answer this question for any different delay he wishes to assume.

To answer the question, I have quantified some of the benefits of some major innovations and the costs that would have been imposed had these been delayed in reaching the market. These innovations cannot of course be duplicated. The purpose of this exercise is simply to establish the magnitude of benefits missed by delaying a typical major innovation. I have examined in retrospect innovations in tuberculosis therapy, tranquilizers, and polio vaccine. I have examined as hypothetical cases two major health problems—cancer and heart disease—which are the focus of much current research, and I have tried to establish the magnitude of the costs of delaying introduction of obviously hypothetical drugs which could substantially mitigate these problems. To provide comparability, each innovation has been treated as if the year it occurred were 1970. These evaluations are deliberately conservative, notably but not exclusively because they do not allow for population and per capita income growth.

Benefits of Past Innovations: Tuberculosis Therapy

Some historical data on tuberculosis are presented in Table 7. The fragmentary data in the last two columns of the table compared with those in column (1) indicate the high proportion of cases which were terminal prior to about 1947. The gradual decline in TB mortality in this period is in large part attributable to reduced communication of the disease through improved sanitation and, especially, early isolation of victims. In the mid-1940s two drugs were discovered, streptomycin and PAS, which acted directly against the tuberculosis bacteria. Their wide distribution, beginning about 1947, and the introduction of isoniazid in 1952 markedly accelerated the decline in the TB mortality rate. More victims were cured early and this, in turn, reduced communication of the disease.

To evaluate the benefits of these drugs, one must first take into account the mortality and morbidity reduction that could have been expected without them. I assume that the mortality rate would have declined by 4.5 percent per year after 1947 had streptomycin and PAS never been introduced. This is roughly the 1920-47 average annual decline, and exceeds the average annual decline for 1900-47. The mortality saving attributable to the new TB drugs in any year

Table 7

TUBERCULOSIS MORTALITY, MORBIDITY AND HOSPITAL ADMISSIONS RATES

(selected periods)

Period	Mortality Rate (per 100,000 per year) (1)	Average Annual Decrease of Mortality Rate from Preceding Period (percent) (2)	Morbidity Rate (cases per 100,000 per year) (3)	Hospital Admissions (per 100,000 per year) (4)
1901–05	181.9	—	—	—
1906–10	164.4	2.0	—	—
1911–15	145.2	2.5	—	—
1916–20	134.1	1.6	—	—
1921–25	91.5	8.0	—	—
1926–30	78.0	3.2	—	—
1931–35	60.3	5.3	—	67.8
1936–40	50.4	3.6	—	74.5
1941–44	42.8	3.7	87.4	71.7
1945–47	36.6	4.6	88.1	68.5
1948–53	21.2	12.9	79.7	71.9
1954–57	8.9	19.0	56.6	66.7e
Year 1969	2.6	9.6	25.4e	27.6e

Note: e indicates "estimate" obtained by splicing a later to an earlier series.
Source: Column (1): U.S. Bureau of the Census, *Historical Statistics of the United States, Colonial Times to 1957* (Washington, D. C.: Government Printing Office, 1960), and *Statistical Abstract of the United States* (Washington, D. C.: Government Printing Office, various issues).

Column (2): Annual percentage change of column (1) between midpoints of periods.

Column (3): 1941-50, U.S. Public Health Service, *Vital Statistics: Special Reports,* vol. 37, no. 9 (Washington, D. C.: Government Printing Office, 1951); 1951–57, U.S. Public Health Service, *Vital Statistics of the United States,* vol. 1 (Washington, D. C.: Government Printing Office, various issues); 1969, *Statistical Abstract.*

Column (4): U.S. Bureau of the Census, *Historical Statistics* and *Statistical Abstract.* Pre- and post-1954 data are derived from reports of the American Hospital Association and American Medical Association, respectively, on number of admissions to tuberculosis hospitals.

is found by reducing the 1947 rate by 4.5 percent per year and then subtracting the actual rate. I assume further that this saving reaches a maximum a decade after introduction of streptomycin and PAS. While the abnormally high rate of decline in mortality has persisted,

Table 8

ESTIMATED COST OF TWO-YEAR DELAY IN INTRODUCING DRUGS FOR TUBERCULOSIS THERAPY

(values as of 1970)

Years after Intro- duction	Mortality Savings of Drugs			Morbidity Savings of Drugs		
	Death rate reduction (per 100,000) (1)	Number of lives saved (thousands) (2)	Discounted value of lives saved ($ millions) (3)	Reduction of incidence (per 100,000) (4)	Number of victims spared (thousands) (5)	Discounted value of earnings for victims spared ($ millions) (6)
1	2.1	4.3	$ 185	0	0	$ 0
2	4.4	9.0	351	0	0	0
3	4.9	10.0	355	5.3	10.8	47
4	8.0	16.3	528	7.5	15.3	60
5	11.1	22.6	665	12.9	26.3	93
6	13.4	27.3	730	15.2	31.0	100
7	14.4	29.3	714	19.1	38.9	114
8	14.5	29.5	653	20.8	42.4	113
9	14.1	28.7	577	25.4	51.7	126
10th and subsequent years	14.1	28.7	5,241	27.7	56.4	1,245
Total			$9,999			$1,898
Total for two-year delay		57.4	8,259		112.8	1,568
Cost of delay			$1,740			$ 330

Note: Column (1) is calculated as 1947 death rate $\times$ (.955)^t — actual death rate, 1948–56.

Column (2) is calculated as column (1) $\times$ 203.7 million, the 1970 population.

Column (3) is calculated as column (2) $\times$ average present value of life saved. This value is computed by estimating the number of lives saved in each age-sex cohort for 1956 and using these numbers as weights to compute a weighted average of cohort lifetime earnings. To estimate the number of lives saved, the 1920-47 decline in the cohort death rate is extrapolated to 1956; the actual 1956 death rate is subtracted and the difference multiplied by cohort population. The weighted average of cohort lifetime earnings is $47,400. The data in column (3) are thus the present value of $47,400 $\times$ column (2). Cohort lifetime earnings are derived from 1970 earnings data. The typical cohort member's age is assumed to be halfway between end points, and he is assumed to earn the median income of his and older cohorts for his expected lifetime. This earning stream is discounted at 10 percent.

Column (4) is calculated as (87.4 — actual incidence) $\times$ .726. The most recent incidence data are for "newly reported active cases," and, for years of overlap with earlier data, these were .726 of total reported cases. For the first two years, this figure is negative, so zero saving is assumed.

Column (5) is calculated as column (4) $\times$ 1970 population.

Column (6) is calculated as column (5) $\times$ present value of one year's average earnings of victim spared. Morbidity is assumed proportional to mortality in each age-sex cohort. Therefore the weights for column (3) are applied to 1970 median earnings in each cohort to compute one year's earnings of victim spared ($5,739). Column (6) is thus the present value of $5,739 $\times$ column (5) at 10 percent.

Source: Figures for morbidity and mortality: See Table 7, columns (1) and (3); earnings: U.S. Bureau of the Census, *Current Population Reports*, series P-60, no. 80 (Washington, D. C.: Government Printing Office, 1971).

61

I assume that the more recent portion of the decline would have been engendered by some potential non-drug-related medical advance, so that any error understates the importance of drugs. Similarly, I assume that drug-related savings from reduced morbidity reached a maximum in 1957.

Morbidity savings would include both increased earnings and reduced medical costs. I assume the latter to be zero. Table 7 indicates that hospital admissions for TB remained essentially unchanged from the mid-1940s to 1957. I have ignored the possibility that the more complete hospitalization for TB victims entailed substitution of lower-cost treatment for out-of-hospital alternatives. The only morbidity savings are therefore the earnings of those who would have been expected to contract TB had streptomycin, isoniazid, and PAS not been introduced. Since the fragmentary data indicate no pre-1947 trend in morbidity or hospital admissions, the expected non-drug morbidity rate is taken to be 87.4, the 1941-44 average, for each year 1948-57.

The resulting estimates of the mortality and morbidity savings attributable to streptomycin, isoniazid, and PAS are given in columns (2) and (5) of Table 8. By 1957, annual mortality and morbidity were reduced by 29,000 and 56,000 (1970 population base), respectively, or to about 40 and 60 percent of the levels expected in the absence of TB drugs. These savings can be converted to money values. Each life saved is evaluated at the discounted value of (1970) median earnings for the "average" life saved, as estimated from the 1956 age-sex distribution of lives saved. This is done to account for the disproportionate number of working males saved. It results in an estimated value per life saved about 20 percent higher than the value implied by U.S. per capita income data. Each TB case prevented is assumed to gain an additional year's earnings, one year being a rough estimate of the term of the typical TB case reported to Weisbrod.[10]

The present value of reduced TB morbidity and mortality (1970 income and population base) is reported in columns (3) and (6) of Table 8. The sum is about $12 billion. The table also shows the present value of the same streams of benefits commencing two years later than they did; the sum is about $10 billion. The $2 billion difference represents the loss in 1970 values that would have been incurred had streptomycin, isoniazid, and PAS been kept from widespread introduction for two years' additional testing and evaluation.[11] The most obvious loss would have been incurred by the 13,300 or so who would have died in those two years. But the less obvious losses—the excess death and morbidity from delayed diffusion of the drugs and delay in their effects on communication of the disease—are quantitatively more important: they amount to a further 44,100 lives lost and 112,800 extra TB victims.

Benefits of Past Innovations: Tranquilizers

The first of the modern tranquilizers, chlorpromazine, was introduced in 1954. Since then, over forty other tranquilizers have been introduced. The group now accounts for more than 10 percent of all prescription drug sales. Many purchasers of these drugs are seeking relief from tension and anxiety symptoms which do not have any easily measurable effects on individual productivity. The drugs have, however, been used for treatment of severe psychoses, and it is on the unusual benefits of the drugs in this use that I have concentrated.

Before the introduction of tranquilizers, severe psychotic disorders often entailed lengthy confinement in a mental hospital. The tranquilizers have not reduced the incidence of these disorders, but have reduced the average length of confinement. That is, the drugs help some psychotics to function in a noninstitutional environment, so that their hospital confinement can be terminated early.[12] The net effect of the tranquilizers has been a substantial reduction in the average length of confinement and a less substantial reduction in total patient-days at mental hospitals.

The basic data are given in Table 9. The absence of any change in the incidence of disabling psychotic disorders is evident from column (1). Both the pre- and post-tranquilizer growth in hospital admission rates is around 2¼ to 2½ percent per year. The average period of confinement was about three years until 1943. This declined to two-and-one-fourth years by 1947, but stayed at that level until chlorpromazine was introduced. Since that time the decline continued largely uninterrupted to the present level of less than one year. The length of the period of decline seems attributable both to a succession of drug innovations and to their gradual acceptance by the medical profession. Most NCEs in the chlorpromazine family (the phenothiazines) were introduced by 1959, but one was introduced as recently as 1970. There was considerable initial skepticism about the effectiveness of the phenothiazines: the major clinical evidence supporting their effectiveness was completed only in the mid-1960s.[13]

This history raises two problems for estimating the benefits of tranquilizers. On both of these I have leaned toward underesti-

Table 9

ANNUAL ADMISSIONS, PATIENT-DAYS AND AVERAGE LENGTH OF STAY, MENTAL HOSPITALS
(selected periods)

Period	Annual Admissions (per 1,000) (1)	Patient-Days (per 1,000) (2)	Average Length of Stay (days per patient) (3)
1932–35	1.4	1,394	1,025
1936–40	1.5	1,573	1,063
1941–45	1.7	1,673	1,014
1946–50	2.0	1,651	817
1951–54	2.0	1,648	817
1955–58	2.2	1,520	697
1959–61	2.3	1,458	626
1962–64	2.6	1,373	522
1969	3.1	958	309

Note: Column (2) is average daily census at mental hospital times number of days in year divided by population.

Column (3) is column (2)/column (1). This is an approximation, since many patients were admitted in prior years.

Source: Columns (1) and (2): U.S. Bureau of the Census, *Historical Statistics* and *Statistical Abstract*.

mating benefits. First, the failure of the decline in average length of stay at mental hospitals to persist beyond 1947 implies that the post-1954 rise in admissions would, in the absence of the tranquilizers, have been accompanied by a rise in patient-days. However, there is no important trend in patient-days from 1936 to 1954. I have assumed that the same would have been true after 1954. This means that in the absence of the tranquilizers, the immediate pre-1954 average of 1.65 patient-days per capita would have been experienced in each post-1954 year. Second, it seems plausible that the full benefits from tranquilizers have not yet been attained. But the further one goes from 1954, the greater the likelihood that, had chlorpromazine not been introduced, some nontranquilizer treatment would have been discovered which produced some of the same benefits. I have therefore arbitrarily assumed that benefits attributable solely to the tranquilizers reached a maximum ten years after chlorpromazine was introduced. The subsequent incremental benefits are assumed to have been attainable by a conjectural alternative.

The benefits from tranquilizers consist of savings in mental hospital expenditures and of earnings for those who would have been confined if tranquilizers were unavailable. These savings are presented in Table 10 using 1970 data. Each mental hospital patient-day saved is assumed to allow earnings of $10.70 (1970 per capita personal income per day) and savings of $16.67 (1970 daily expenses per patient at mental hospitals) in hospital costs. While it seems surprising, the value of the savings from tranquilizers is virtually identical to that of the TB drugs, and so the cost of a two-year delay in their introduction would have been the same. However, unlike TB drugs, tranquilizer costs are not negligible, since patients must frequently use them for long periods following hospital confinement and the drugs are fairly expensive.

Table 10

ESTIMATED SAVINGS FROM TRANQUILIZERS
(values as of 1970)

Years After Introduction	Patient-Days Saved (millions) (1)	Present Value of Savings ($ millions) (2)
1	1.02	$ 25.3
2	13.44	303.3
3	42.17	865.4
4	49.70	927.6
5	40.13	680.0
6	32.39	499.3
7	44.61	625.4
8	51.13	651.2
9	52.35	606.5
10th and subsequent years	66.00 per year	6,944.2
Total		$12,128.2
Total for two-year delay		10,017.8
Cost of delay	132.10	$ 2,110.4

Note: Column (1) is calculated as (1.650 − patient-days in mental hospitals per capita in years 1955-64) × 1970 population.

Column (2) is calculated as $27.33 × column (1) discounted to present at 10 percent. $27.33 = 1970 daily personal income per capita ($10.70) + 1970 daily per patient expenditures at mental hospitals ($16.63).

Source: U.S. Bureau of the Census, *Statistical Abstract*.

One can make a generous estimate of the magnitude of these drug costs. Assume that each mental hospital admittee, whether or not he is susceptible to tranquilizer treatment, becomes committed to lifetime maintenance phenothiazine therapy. I take $600 as the present value of the cost of this commitment.[14] For the 1955 hospital admission rate and 1970 population, this would entail a cost of $268.8 million in the first year following introduction of tranquilizers. Discounting this in perpetuity at 7½ percent (10 percent minus 2½ percent annual increase in hospital admissions per capita) yields a present value of $3,584 million. A slightly smaller figure is obtained by discounting at 7½ percent the total 1970 retail value of in- and out-of-hospital sales of all tranquilizers used as antipsychotics.[15] This assumes, hyperbolically, that all these tranquilizers are prescribed exclusively for present and former mental patients. When this crude cost estimate is deducted from gross tranquilizer savings, we are left with net benefits of about $8 billion and a net cost for delay in introduction of about $1.4 billion.[16] This would correspond to 132.1 million extra patient-days in mental hospitals, or an average of twenty-five extra days for each admittee over a period of twelve years.

Benefits of Past Innovations: Polio Vaccines

The Salk vaccine has permitted the virtual eradication of polio. For this reason, it is commonly regarded as among the most important innovations in modern medicine. Yet the economic value of polio vaccine does not come close to that of either innovation previously discussed. I rely for this conclusion mainly on Weisbrod's recent study of the costs and benefits of polio vaccines and will summarize his results here.[17]

Weisbrod estimated that the rate of return to research and development on polio vaccine was about 11 percent per year. (This is the rate which equates the cost of pre-1956 research and development to the value of post-1956 benefits.) Given Weisbrod's estimates of pre-1956 R&D expenses, the present value of post-1956 benefits implied by this rate of return is about $60 million, and this can be doubled for 1970 incomes and prices. Had a law like the 1962 amendments delayed introduction of Salk vaccine by two years, about $20 million of these benefits would have been lost. This is clearly a trivial sum next to those derived for TB drugs and tranquilizers, and it is useful to explore the reasons for this difference in order of magnitude.

Incidence and mortality. Weisbrod estimates a no-vaccine incidence of 36,000 polio cases per year, which is roughly the average incidence for the decade prior to 1956. By contrast, there were over 100,000 TB cases per year and over 300,000 admissions to mental hospitals per year at the time the relevant drug innovations occurred. Something like 5 percent of all polio cases terminated in death, as compared with more than one-third of TB cases. Moreover, a large fraction of polio deaths occurred among the very young, whose discounted future earnings are relatively low. Thus, the aggregate mortality cost of polio was far lower than that of TB before the introduction of the relevant drugs.

Morbidity cost. The high incidence of polio among the young entails a substantially smaller sacrifice of earnings per day of disability than for TB or psychotic disorders. At the same time, many polio cases were nonparalytic and these involved relatively low treatment costs. Weisbrod estimates the average treatment cost per case at $550 in 1950 prices. By contrast, each 1950 mental hospital admission cost about $2,000 (800 days of confinement at about $2.50 per day) and each 1950 TB hospital admission cost about $1,750 (250 days at $7 per day).

Drug application cost. Eradication of polio was achieved by vaccinating the bulk of the population alive in the mid-1950s, and then the bulk of subsequent newborn. The capital outlay for this massive initial vaccination (Weisbrod estimates it at $350-$625 million) has been amortized by benefits accruing over a long period to a small fraction of those immunized. This ubiquitous and immediate expenditure offsets most of the benefits of the Salk vaccine. The interest cost of the initial mass vaccination is about $1,000 per polio case prevented (at a 10 percent rate), while Weisbrod estimates a gross benefit of $1,350 per case prevented. Neither TB nor psychotic disorders entailed this kind of capital outlay to implement drug therapy.

I have independently calculated the net benefits of polio vaccine according to the methods I used for TB drugs and tranquilizers. Many of the data for the calculation were drawn from an AMA study which employs substantially higher treatment cost estimates than does Weisbrod.[18] When allowance is made for the prodigious secular increase in hospital costs, these data yield 1970 net benefit estimates considerably above Weisbrod's, though they do not obviate the conclusions to be drawn from his data. I will only outline the procedure I used here.[19]

The AMA study provides estimates of the number of polio cases prevented by age from 1955 through 1961. Since the disease was virtually eradicated by 1961, I assumed subsequent benefits and costs equal to those for 1961. The benefits for each case prevented consist of treatment costs saved and earnings permitted. For that portion of cases in which death could have been expected, earnings permitted are taken as the present value of age-cohort lifetime earnings (Weisbrod employs earnings permitted less consumption). For the remainder of cases, I assumed that earnings would have been lost only over the period of hospital confinement, thereby understating savings for cases which involve long-term impairment of productivity. The AMA data on the vaccination status of the population from 1957 to 1961 and on total 1955-1961 vaccination cost are used to estimate vaccination costs in each year to 1961: post-1961 costs are assumed to be .018 (the current birth rate) of the 1955-1961 total each year. I arbitrarily impute a value of $1.50 to the working time forgone by adults to obtain each vaccination. These assumptions result in a present value of benefits less vaccination costs slightly under $900 million, and a cost of a two-year delay in introduction of about $150 million spread over 70,000 additional polio cases. While this is a much larger dollar-cost estimate than Weisbrod's data permit, it is still much smaller than the cost of delaying introduction of something like TB drugs or tranquilizers.

There are some general conclusions suggested by this analysis of drug innovations. First, technological and economic importance can differ substantially. Salk vaccine ranked higher than either streptomycin or chlorpromazine (the ranks were 3, 5 and 7 respectively) on a medical experts' list of the thirty most important drugs introduced between 1934 and 1962 [20] but the latter two are substantially more important economically. Second, we can give some empirical content to the obvious criteria for an economically important innovation—it must successfully treat a malady that has widespread incidence and leads to high mortality or long disability. Given current earnings and hospital costs, any malady which disables more than 50,000 for more than a year each year, or kills more than 5,000 each year, will have an annual dollar cost running into the hundreds of millions.[21] A drug which can materially reduce these figures is bound to generate net benefits far in excess of those generated by typical new drugs, unless it entails continual mass application. Finally, if the 1962 drug amendments delay introduction of any such drug for anything like two years, the cost will be substantial. For example, had introduction of the three drugs analyzed here been delayed that long, the current annual equivalent social cost [22] would have been over $300 million, a sum sufficient roughly to double the previously estimated cost of the 1962 amendments.

Hypothetical Potential Benefits Illustrated

This last point may be illuminated further by data on the two leading causes of death—heart disease and cancer. Both are the subject of extensive pharmacological research, but have so far resisted major medical advances. The best that has been accomplished is a slowing or halting of gradually rising death rates.[23] The two diseases alone account for more than half of all deaths, and it is hardly surprising that their economic cost is enormous. A recent study estimates their cost for the single year 1962 at over $40 billion.[24] Given subsequent inflation, the equivalent today would be more than $50 billion. For this study I have made independent estimates (discussed below) of the present value of the costs that can be expected from these diseases. These employ the conservative estimates of the value of lifetime earnings used previously, but the 1970 annual equivalent cost of these illnesses is still $34 billion.

It is, of course, absurd to believe that any pharmaceutical innovation would instantly abolish these diseases. But clearly any innovation which makes noticeable inroads will generate substantial benefits, and any material delay in introducing that innovation will be extremely costly. The actual costs and benefits must of course be conjectural, but some notion of the quantities involved should be useful.

To obtain this notion, I have first estimated the present expected value of the costs of these diseases if no major therapeutic advance were to occur.[25] The estimates assume that, if there were no significant medical advance, the post-1950 trend in the death rate for each disease in each age-sex cohort would be maintained until 1980, after which the death rate would remain constant.[26] The number of deaths expected in each age-sex cohort in each year was computed for the 1970 cohort population, multiplied by the estimated cost per death, and discounted to 1970. The cost per death has both a mortality and morbidity component. The mortality component is the same discounted value of lifetime earnings for a cohort member that was used in the TB calculations. Morbidity costs consist of current earnings losses and treatment costs for those currently disabled by the disease.[27]

The resulting estimates are given on line 1 of Table 11. They show a total expected cost of about $340 billion for both diseases, with about two-thirds of the total attributable to heart disease. I next assumed that new drugs were discovered which would begin to reduce these costs in 1970. I assumed that any hypothetical drug would reduce the mortality rate (and associated mortality and morbidity costs) gradually over time and achieve maximum effectiveness in 1980. The savings from hypothetical drugs of varying maximum effectiveness are estimated on lines 2 through 5 of Table

Table 11

COSTS FROM HEART DISEASE AND CANCER AND POTENTIAL BENEFITS FROM REDUCING THEIR INCIDENCE

Source of Cost or Benefit (present values, 1970)	Heart Disease		Cancer	
	Millions of dollars	Thousands of lives	Millions of dollars	Thousands of lives
1. Expected costs, no innovations	$222,379		$118,820	
Expected savings due to innovations which reduce mortality in 1980 by:				
2. 10 percent	14,237		7,799	
3. 25 percent	35,694		19,498	
4. 50 percent	71,188		38,996	
5. 75 percent	106,782		58,494	
Expected costs of two-year delay in introducing innovations that would reduce mortality in 1980 by:				
2'. 10 percent	2,478	153.0	1,357	66.5
3'. 25 percent	6,193	382.6	3,393	166.3
4'. 50 percent	12,388	765.2	6,786	332.6
5'. 75 percent	18,580	1,147.7	10,179	499.0

Note: See text for sources and description. Innovations which would reduce the mortality rate are assumed to be introduced in 1970, and the indicated reduction in 1980 is assumed to be attained linearly. For example, in the case of innovations which would reduce mortality rates by 10 percent by 1980, it is assumed that the mortality rate reduction in 1970 is 10/11 percent of the expected 1980 mortality rate, in 1971, 20/11 percent, and so on. The calculations assume an unchanged ratio of mortality to incidence.

11. Thus, a 1970 cancer drug which gradually reduced mortality so that the 1980 rate was 25 percent less than expected would save $19.5 billion (line 3). To put these figures in context, the $12 billion estimated savings from TB drugs (Table 9) came from a tenth year reduction in the mortality rate of about two-thirds from the expected rate. Table 11 indicates that a similarly potent heart disease drug or cancer drug would produce savings well over $71 billion or $39 billion, respectively, before deduction of drug costs.

Finally, we may estimate the costs of delaying the introduction of any hypothetical innovation by two years. The relevant estimates are on line 2'-5' of Table 11, and are based on the assumption that the streams of annual benefits are each pushed forward two years. The delay in introducing even a moderately effective innovation will have costs of several billion dollars and upwards of 100,000 lives. Moreover, one can have greater confidence in these delay-cost estimates than in the total savings estimates from which they are derived. No charge is made against the savings estimates for costs of developing the innovation, so total benefits are overstated. However, by the time an innovation is developed, the development costs have already been incurred. The true costs of delay are simply the gross benefits sacrificed by not using the drug. Lines 2'-5' overstate this only by the direct cost of applying the innovation. If the TB experience is indicative, this cost is likely to be comparatively minor.

Summary and Conclusions

The effects of the 1962 amendments on drug safety and major drug innovations are difficult to ascertain, and it would be misleading to assign single values to their costs and benefits. There have been no new-drug disasters in the decade since the amendments were passed, but the one obvious candidate for that title occurred fully a decade before 1962. There have been no revolutionary therapeutic innovations since 1962 either, but this is not peculiar to the United States.

The safest conclusion that can be drawn is that the amendments have not produced significant safety benefits so far, nor have they foreclosed or delayed extraordinary therapeutic advance. Since the relevant costs and benefits are therefore prospective, we are limited to estimating plausible magnitudes for these if they are realized. I have done this, first, by assuming that future innovations will repeat the past (not of course in their pharmacology but in the number of people they will affect) and, second, by trying to put plausible bounds on the potential effect of the amendments on innovation in two major current research areas. While none of the resulting estimates involves an innovation directly affected by the amendments, a fairly clear pattern emerges. The 1962 amendments assume implicitly that it is worth sacrificing some potential return from an innovation in order to gain reduced risk. Our estimates suggest that if any trade would be profitable, it would be more risk for more return.

One of three innovations examined (Salk vaccine) turns out to have had small net economic benefits. But both of the others have benefits very much larger than those captured by the developers. In the one case (tranquilizers) where drug manufacturers have reaped substantial profits, annual sales at retail—which of course exceed profits—do not come close to exhausting half the measurable benefits. If the prospective failure to reap a substantial part of the benefits delayed the introduction of these drugs for even a brief time, the benefits missed could easily have been on the order of several hundred million dollars. It is equally true that, given corporate limited liability and the costs of using the courts, innovators may not bear all the costs of a drug disaster. But, in fact, disasters are neither so frequent nor so severe as to begin to offset the gains from major innovations. To put the matter baldly, if generally greater risk taking had hastened the marketing of TB drugs by six months, the number of lives saved directly (that is, excluding the effects of reduced communication of TB and hastier diffusion of the drug) would have been three times as great as all those lost to the delayed discovery of the lethal effects of chloramphenicol.[28]

I am unaware of any data that shed light on the question whether the benefits from greater haste might in fact have been purchased at a cost smaller than a tripled incidence of major drug disasters. However, if empirical support for the proposition that there was too little risk taking before 1962 is lacking, the data then available emphatically fail to support the contrary proposition embodied in the amendments. The amendments have produced less haste. Even if the future number of major therapeutic advances were unaffected, this change would be costly. It would, for example, require the prevention of more than one chloramphenicol incident annually to offset the direct cost in lives lost because of a two-year delay of a once-in-a-decade innovation like the TB drugs. A similar comparison between something like the tranquilizers and chloramphenicol cannot be this direct, since a tradeoff between lives and disability is involved. However, the more-than-fiftyfold difference between the cost of a two-year delay in introducing something like tranquilizers and the total cost of excess chloramphenicol deaths indicates how great the pessimism about safety of unregulated drugs or the nonmeasurable value of life must be for the prospective benefits of the amendments to offset their costs.

These conclusions hold even when we consider the potential costs of a thalidomide tragedy in its most virulent form and on the most extreme interpretation of its costs—that malformation is the equivalent of death. My high estimate of the economic cost (or cost in "lives" lost) of such a hypothetical tragedy is well below that of a one-year, let alone two-year, delay in marketing either the TB drugs or the phenothiazines. Moreover, it should be remembered that these do not nearly exhaust the major innovations of the pre-1962 period, while it would be difficult to expect anything like a thalidomide tragedy more than once a decade. It is interesting in this connection that the high estimate of the cost of a hypothetical birth-defects outbreak is roughly equal to the benefit of a three-month speed-up in the introduction of the three beneficial innovations discussed here. If one views the outbreak of birth defects as the likely consequence of any relaxed (pre-1962) safety regulation which would permit the three-month speed-up to be attained for all drugs, it may be concluded that there was almost surely too little risk taking before 1962, not to mention *since* 1962.

This conclusion is further reinforced when it is recalled that the measurable prospective benefit of eliminating all chloramphenicol and thalidomide tragedies falls well short of the measurable cost of the amendments in benefits forgone on the ordinary new drugs whose development they discourage. This net loss may be further exacerbated by modest delays in introducing unusually beneficial new drugs. It is worth emphasizing that such delay is intrinsic in the regulatory procedure required by the amendments. When one considers the prospective payoff for innovation in the treatment of something like heart disease or cancer, the potential cost of delay becomes awesome. Should only a moderately successful innovation in the treatment of either disease come within the ambit of the amendments, our estimate that their cost is something like a 5- to 10-percent drug excise tax will prove egregiously low. And even the data on innovations in the treatment of less widespread diseases will indicate how extravagant is the cost of reduced risk built into the amendments.

CHAPTER VI

EFFECT OF THE
1962 AMENDMENTS ON THE
WEALTH OF DRUG PRODUCERS

The effects we have traced to the 1962 amendments have conflicting implications for the wealth of drug producers. On the one hand, the amendments have raised the cost of innovation and reduced the demand for it. On the other hand, they have erected a barrier to new competition for producers of established drugs, and made the demand for the output of the established producers higher than it would otherwise be. The producer who specializes in new drugs will be hurt and the producer who specializes in old drugs will be helped. However, the typical drug firm produces both new and old drugs, and the net effect of the amendments on this typical firm is ambiguous.

In an attempt to resolve the ambiguity I have compared the fortunes of an investor in a representative group of drug producers after the amendments with what could have been expected in their absence. Unfortunately for this purpose, the typical drug producer does not sell only in the U.S. prescription drug market, so the effect of the amendments will inevitably be obscured by conditions in foreign or non-drug markets. The best we can do is to focus on those firms which have a significant fraction of their sales affected by the amendments.

There have, of course, been other changes in the domestic drug market which have affected the wealth of drug producers, and these too must be accounted for. For example, no one familiar with the stock market will be surprised to learn that drug stocks have out-performed the market since 1962. An investor in the group of drug stocks I use here would have been about 50 percent wealthier in 1971 by investing in them than if he had invested an equal amount in the average of other industrial stocks in 1962 (assuming reinvestment of all dividends). But drug stocks also generally outperformed the market before 1962, so that their post-1962 performance alone cannot yield conclusive implications for the effect of the amendments.

It nevertheless appears safe to conclude that drug producers have not as a group been hurt by the amendments. The basis for this conclusion is elaborated in the appendix, but it can be stated succinctly here:

(1) The superior pre-1962 performance of drug stocks can be traced to persistently superior growth of drug sales relative to general economic growth.

(2) The degree of superiority in both drug stock performance and drug market growth after 1962 is substantially the same as before 1962.

Some of the relevant data are in Table 12. The first two lines of the table show what would be the average annual growth in the wealth of investors who committed their resources entirely to drug stocks and the average annual growth in the wealth of those who committed their resources to a diversified list of stocks (the "market"). In both cases that growth has slowed since 1962, but the difference between the performance of drug stocks and the performance of the general market has remained virtually the same: the drug investor is better off by about 5 percent per year on average. Now, in the pre-1962 period, it turned out that for each percentage point by which growth in drug sales exceeded that of GNP in any year, drug stocks outperformed the market by something over two percentage points (see Appendix, Table A-3). Lines 4 through 6 of Table 12 contain data on drug market and GNP growth, and these reflect the relationship to the stock market just noted. That is, before 1962 drug sales growth exceeded GNP growth by a margin about half that of the margin of drug stock performance over the market, and this pre-1962 experience was almost exactly duplicated in the post-1962 decade. In other words, the reward to the investor with foresight to know in 1962 that drug sales would continue to grow faster than the economy does not seem to have been diminished by the working of the amendments.

This is not, however, to say that the amendments have had no effects on the wealth of owners of the drug industry. They appear rather to have had offsetting effects. On the one hand, because of the cost and demand effects of the amendments the specific return to any innovation has been reduced. The stock market has not greeted the typical post-1962 innovation with as much enthusiasm as it displayed for its pre-1962 counterpart. But innovation is also

76

Table 12

RATES OF RETURN FOR DRUG STOCKS AND STANDARD AND POOR'S INDUSTRIALS, AND ASSOCIATED DATA
(selected periods)

Datum	Period 1949–61	Period 1962–71
Average compound annual rate of return:		
1. Drug stocks	23.0%	12.3%
2. Standard & Poor's Industrials	17.7	7.7
3. Difference (line 1 − line 2)	5.3	4.6
Average compound annual rate of growth (constant dollars):		
4. Drug sales	5.6	6.0
5. Gross national product	3.2	3.9
6. Difference (line 4 − line 5)	2.4	2.1
Difference between return in one year on drug stocks and Standard and Poor's Industrials:		
7. Highest difference in period	33.4	18.3
8. Lowest difference in period	− 11.9	− 7.5
9. Range (line 7 − line 8)	45.3	25.8

Note: Line 1 is the average annual wealth change (that is, capital gains plus dividends) as a percent of wealth at the start of each year for an investor concentrating his wealth on drug stocks. The investor is assumed to sell his holdings each year and reinvest the proceeds along with dividends equally among all drug stocks used in the calculations. These drug stocks are listed in the note to appendix Table A-3. Tax and transactions costs are not included.

Line 2 is the average annual percentage wealth change for an investor who buys a "share" of Standard and Poor's Industrial Stock Price Index and reinvests all dividends.

Lines 4 and 5 are the average compound annual growth in drug sales and gross national product, measured in constant 1958 dollars.

The data on lines 7, 8 and 9 are obtained by subtracting in each year the percentage wealth change for the investor in Standard and Poor's Industrials from that for an investor in five drug stocks, where data are available for each year 1949–71 (these are Abbott, American Home Products, Merck, Pfizer, and Smith, Kline and French). Line 7 shows the highest such difference in each period and line 8 the lowest.

Source: See Appendix, Table A-3.

a competitive weapon which makes existing products obsolete or, as we have seen, stimulates price reductions on existing products. This indirect effect of innovation, reducing the wealth of the innovator's rivals, has occurred less frequently since 1962 than before. On balance, the increase in owner wealth from the greater protection which the amendments afford the market position of established drugs has offset the impact of reduced returns to each innovation. (The data relevant to this conclusion are discussed in the appendix.)

The amendments have had an additional favorable effect on drug company owners, not on the level of their wealth, but on its year-to-year variability. A concomitant of reduced innovation is reduced opportunity for one firm to experience unusually large gains from innovation or losses from obsolescence. We would therefore expect the amendments to have worked to reduce the year-to-year variability of the returns to the owners of the typical drug company, and to compress the differences in returns among companies in any year. Moreover, since pre-1962 innovation tended to be cyclical, the year-to-year variability of returns to drug company owners treated as a group should also have been reduced.

These anticipated effects are borne out by the data. There are five sample companies (listed in Table 12) whose returns can be traced through the whole 1949-71 period. A crude measure of the relative variability of annual returns to an investor who kept equal dollar amounts invested in each of them is provided on lines 7, 8 and 9 of Table 12. These show the range of this investor's experience relative to the market in each period—the greatest excess over returns in the rest of the market in any one year and the greatest deficit. The data reveal that this range becomes substantially more compressed after 1962. Both the best and worst experience are closer to that in the rest of the market after 1962. This same pattern shows up in the individual company returns. For four of the five companies (Abbott is the exception), the best pre-1962 relative return exceeds its post-1962 counterpart. For three of the five (Pfizer and Smith, Kline, and French are the exceptions), the worst pre-1962 relative return is worse than the worst post-1962 return. For all five, the range of relative returns (best minus worst) is more compressed after 1962. Finally, differences in annual returns among the five companies also narrowed. The difference between the highest return in a year and the lowest averages 47.5 percent before 1962 and 37.6 percent after 1962.[1]

It seems clear that the volatility of drug stocks, individually and collectively, has been reduced since 1962. The significance of this lies in the apparent preference which investors usually have for reduced volatility. Historically, they seem to have tended to accept a smaller return on less volatile securities.[2] However, there has been no deterioration in the return on drug stocks relative to the return on other stocks since 1962, while at the same time these returns have become less variable relative to those on other stocks. Since drug company owners have obtained this greater stability of wealth for "free," one may conclude that the amendments have yielded them net benefits. It is difficult to measure the precise value of these benefits, but a highly tentative estimate of $200 million annually is developed in the appendix.

CHAPTER VII

SUMMARY AND CONCLUDING REMARKS

The main conclusions on the benefits and costs of the 1962 drug amendments are here briefly restated with substantial rounding of dollar amounts.

Treated as a group, consumers seem clearly to have lost on balance from the amendments. Their annual gains and losses break down as follows:

(1) missed benefits (consumer surplus) from the reduced flow of new drugs, producing a loss of $300-400 million;

(2) reduced waste on purchases of ineffective new drugs, producing a gain of under $100 million; and

(3) higher prices for existing drugs because of reduced competition from new drugs, producing a loss of $50 million.

These measurable effects add up to a net loss of $250 to $350 million, or about 6 percent of total drug sales. There are additional gains from the screening, through added testing, of especially unsafe new drugs from the market and additional losses from delay in marketing especially beneficial innovations. Since neither type has been proposed or marketed since 1962 and their probable incidence without the amendments is difficult to measure, the gains and losses must be conjectural. If an incidence of one of each type per decade is assumed, and the amendments are assumed to eliminate all especially unsafe drugs, the gain is well under $50 million and the loss about $200 million annually. The latter figure is conservative, given the rate at which unusually beneficial drugs were introduced before 1962 and the magnitude of existing major health problems.

Drug producers as a group seem neither to have been helped nor hurt by the amendments, the gains of reduced competition having been roughly balanced by the added costs of innovation. However, the amendments appear to have reduced variability in the growth of their wealth. If it is assumed that, everything else being equal, drug company owners prefer the reduced variability, the highly tentative value of the resulting gain is $200 million.

If the Food, Drug and Cosmetics Act was intended to benefit consumers, the inescapable conclusion to which this study points is that the intent is better served by reversion to the status quo ante 1962. This conclusion follows directly from the size of the problem with which the 1962 amendments sought to cope. Consumer losses from purchases of ineffective drugs or hastily marketed unsafe drugs appear to have been trivial compared to gains from innovation. In this context, any perceptible deterrent to innovation was bound to impose net losses on consumers. The amendments clearly provided such a deterrent. Indeed, the conclusion can be put more strongly. If our estimates of the gains and losses from exceptionally beneficial and unsafe drugs, respectively, are at all reasonable, there was already a costly bias in the pre-1962 proof-of-safety requirement. If relaxation of that requirement would have compressed the new-drug development process only slightly, the resulting gains would have left a margin of lives saved and disability avoided that would more than have offset increased losses from unsafe drugs. The risk-return tradeoff was already biased against drug consumers in 1962. The amendments have simply exaggerated the bias.

It is easier to state our conclusion than it is to be sanguine about the prospects for reduced regulation of drug innovation. Since the 1962 amendments do not appear to have benefitted any substantial group and have hurt some, one might question their political viability. However, the most important group that has been hurt, drug consumers, cannot be expected to offer effective pressure for change. The damage to each member of this group can be little more than a few dollars per year, so that the members of the group have little incentive to bear the costs of political organization. Moreover, reduced regulation of the quality of any consumer good sharply contradicts the thrust of most organized groups that today purport to promote the consumer interest. One organized group that might share in the gains from reduced regulation of drug innovation is the American Medical Association, but the AMA has not taken a strong position on the matter since the Kefauver hearings when it testified against requiring proof of efficacy for drug advertising. Finally, our results indicate that the producer group which has benefitted from the amendments may be at least as large as that which has been hurt: coherent support for reduced regulation cannot confidently be anticipated from producer groups.

If there will be no substantial reduction of the formal restraints embodied in the amendments, it is unlikely any substantial reduction in the costs they have generated will be accomplished by purely administrative changes. The FDA is, after all, confronted by the same political forces that favor legislative inertia. In addition, the FDA can expect little of the reward for extremely successful innovations, but substantial cost for wrongly certifying an unsafe or ineffective drug. Surely, no FDA official who has assisted the speedy introduction of a highly beneficial drug has received anything remotely resembling the public accolades accorded the colleague who prevented marketing of thalidomide. Exhorting the FDA to speed up the NDA process or to reduce its information requirements is not likely to be very fruitful. And it would be misleading to seek the source of the inefficiency of drug regulation in the detail of FDA procedures. The important conclusions of this study are that, perhaps before and certainly after 1962, too many resources have been devoted to testing of drug safety and efficacy before marketing and that, unless the law requiring proof of efficacy is rescinded, continued resource waste is inevitable. A favorable change in FDA procedures could reduce, but could never eliminate, the waste commanded by the law.

EPILOGUE

THE FDA'S REPLY
TO THIS STUDY

The main results of the research upon which this study is based were presented at a conference held by the Center for Policy Study, University of Chicago, in December 1972. They received wide publicity, notably in a *Newsweek* column by Milton Friedman.[1] Shortly thereafter, Senator Gaylord Nelson of Wisconsin convened hearings on the regulation of prescription drug innovation before his Monopoly Subcommittee of the Senate Small Business Committee. These results were discussed further at those hearings. The Nelson hearings provided the forum in which the FDA chose to reply officially to the points raised in this study and to other criticisms of the existing state of new-drug regulation.

A brief summary of the FDA's reply cannot do it full justice, though it is to be hoped my summary will not do it violence either.[2] Unsurprisingly, the FDA's reply was substantially an unqualified defense of the existing regulatory framework. In part, this defense was based on an emphatic recital of the benefits from improved drug safety and efficacy. Except for its lack of discussion of the costs of these benefits, this part of the FDA's reply only embellished points made in this study.

The more important part of the FDA's testimony, for present purposes, concerned the post-amendment decline in innovation. In this, the FDA sought both exculpation and credit for the decline. It pointed out that the decline began before 1962 and extends beyond the United States, so that something other than the 1962 amendments must have contributed to it. At the same time, Henry Simmons, director of the FDA's Bureau of Drugs and its chief witness before the Nelson committee, asked the critics of the current regulatory system to "acknowledge that in many respects, this [decline] may be a good sign and ultimately of benefit to the American people. After all, most of this decrease is accounted for by the marked decline in marketing of [drugs] . . . considered by experts to be incompatible with the practice of sound therapeutics." [3]

This last claim was embellished by a listing of the number of "truly important, significant and unique therapeutic entities" which "has remained relatively stable for the past 22 years, numbering approximately 5 to 7 drugs per year." [4] Thus, the post-1962 decline in drug innovation has not, according to the FDA, been accompanied by a decline in "truly important" drug innovation. The FDA's listing does not entirely support its point. The annual average of FDA-designated "truly important" drugs is 7.1 for 1950-1962 and 5.8 subsequently, although it is true that the difference between these two figures is not statistically significant. Even if the FDA reply did support its point, the apparent subjectiveness of the criteria according to which the listing was developed invites difficulty in confirming the FDA's result. For example, an unpublished version of the same FDA listing reveals an annual average of 12.3 "important therapeutic advances" for 1950-62 and 9.1 for 1963-70—a difference which is statistically significant.

Perhaps in recognition of these difficulties, the FDA sought further support for its contention that its regulation of new drugs does not deny the consumer substantial benefits. The point was made that, while many new drugs are sold abroad but not domestically, only a very few of these are sold in more than one or two countries. Since one might expect important therapeutic advances to gain a universal market, the failure of most foreign new drugs to accomplish this is, on this argument, implicit testimony of their lack of importance. Conversely, the fact that most new drugs which penetrate several foreign markets also are sold in the United States implies that American regulation does not deny consumers access to important new drugs. Finally, the FDA pointed to the continued willingness of United States drug producers to devote growing amounts to new-drug research and development as evidence that market opportunities for important new drugs have not been significantly foreclosed.

I believe it is more important to compare the FDA's evaluation of the decline in drug innovation with the evaluation contained in this study than it is to review in detail the role of the amendments in producing that decline. Suffice it to say that the careful reader of this study will not find all the decline in drug innovation from the peak level of the late 1950s attributed to the working of the amendments. What I have contended in Chapter II is that it would have been reasonable, in light of post-1962 drug market growth and foreign experience, to have expected an innovation rate roughly equal to the average of the decade before the amendments (an average which is roughly two-thirds of the peak). The actual post-1962 rate has been roughly 60 percent below that average.

For a decline of this magnitude to be regarded as "a good sign and ultimately of benefit to the American people," we must believe that the pre-amendment regulatory environment produced substantial numbers of ineffective drugs and that the amendments have been highly selective in screening these out. Even if one assumes the selectivity, the belief in the substantial number of ineffective drugs is untenable. It is difficult to conclude that much more than 10 percent of pre-1962 drug purchases went for ineffective drugs. This figure is suggested by the sales of those drugs which the FDA itself has indicated it will remove from the market as a result of the drug-efficacy review conducted by the National Academy of Sciences-National Research Council.[5] A similar estimate (9.4 percent) is obtained by Jondrow in his study of the NAS-NRC review.[6] Finally, it will be recalled that the pessimistic interpretation of *AMA Drug Evaluations* in Chapter IV permitted 20 percent of 1960-62 new drugs to be classed as ineffective in some degree (see Table 5). But when the decline in sales of these drugs over time is taken into account, their sales in an average year also amount to about 10 percent of the total for all 1960-62 new drugs. It appears that a form of "shot-gun therapy" has been applied to the problem of ineffective drugs: for the sake of excising (part of) the potentially offending 10 percent, 60 percent of potential innovation is eliminated. The results of this study are hardly surprising in light of the odds against the success of this therapy.

The heart of the FDA's defense of the current regulatory framework involves a blurring of the distinction between an effective new drug and one which marks a "truly important significant" advance. Indeed, it is striking how far one can go in accepting the FDA's defense without obviating the conclusions reached in this study. It will be recalled that I assumed that any drug which promises benefits substantially greater than those of the "ordinary" new drug would not be kept from the market by the operation of the amendments. The FDA's basic contention is that this assumption corresponds to reality.

There is, of course, no sharp demarcation between the "truly important" new drug and its more mundane counterparts. Nevertheless, it is clear that the majority of new drugs has never been therapeutically revolutionary. Any one of these drugs will ordinarily bring only a modest improvement over existing therapy. However, multiplied twenty-five-fold each year, the resulting benefits accumulate impressively and their denial will represent a nontrivial burden on the consumer. It was sufficient in this study to assume (along with the FDA) that none of the drugs whose development is discouraged by the amendments would have been atypically beneficial. The assumption allowed us to estimate the burden of the amendments at upwards of one-quarter billion dollars annually. The fact that this loss is widely diffused among consumers may make it easy to ignore and politically tolerable, but it does not eliminate it.

My assumption that the amendments have left the most important individual innovations unaffected was methodological. It should be mentioned that its substance has been challenged, notably by Wardell in the works previously cited. However, it is unclear what the link may be between the amendments and the worldwide failure to produce innovations that markedly reduce mortality or morbidity.

There is, however, a wider issue which this worldwide failure has so far relieved Congress from confronting. It is brought into focus by the FDA's contention "that no known [regulatory] approach [promises] shorter, less expensive ways to create safe and effective drugs." [7] This notion that the relevant choice is between "safe and effective" drugs and "unsafe and ineffective" drugs unfortunately pervades the discussion of existing regulation. In this case, much more than pedantry is served by pointing out that the relevant choice is in fact between more and less risk and that a reduction in risk is always costly.

A failure to recognize these facts will lead to a persistent intolerance of risk and a bias against innovation. Indeed, the least expensive way to assure that drugs will be safe and effective— measured by direct expense only—is to tolerate no innovation and rely completely on the tried and true. But in a wider perspective, any attempt to minimize risk in this area has costs which (according to the history of drug innovation) far exceed the benefits: those who will suffer death and disease while a potential drug therapy is evaluated will suffer no less than the victims of a drug disaster, but their number is likely to be much larger than the number of victims of the disaster. The case for present regulatory policy becomes highly dubious if the benefits of risk taking are given the same recognition as the potential costs.

The unequal emphasis placed on the benefits and costs of risk taking may be explained, if not excused, by the contrast between the anonymity of the beneficiaries and the visibility of the victims. A recent example, taken from Wardell, illustrates this point.[8] He cites the case of a benzodiazepine hypnotic (nitrazepam) which was approved for marketing in the United States in 1971, but was available abroad five years earlier. One advantage of this drug over other hypnotics is its safety in overdosage. From data on foreign market penetration of nitrazepam and U.S. deaths from overdosage of hypnotics, Wardell concludes that the five-year delay in U.S. marketing cost over 1,200 lives. Since three times that many died from hypnotic overdosage, the specific identity of the victims of this delay will never be known.

If Wardell's data are anywhere close to the mark, this one obscure incident has cost more lives than the widely publicized chloramphenicol tragedy. Wardell concludes that "introduction of a new drug that *produced* fatalities anywhere approaching this magnitude would be regarded as a major disaster, but the undoubted occurrence of deaths through *failure* to introduce a drug has so far gone unremarked." It is this fact, rather than the particulars of the case, that should temper optimistic appraisals of current regulatory policy.

If it is misleading to seek the specific victims of present regulatory policy, it is equally misleading to personalize the blame for their plight. The FDA framed its defense of present policy as a reply to critics of the performance of its bureaucracy. There may well be room for argument about that performance, but in my own testimony before the Nelson Committee, I attempted to point out that the most well intentioned and effective administration of the 1962 amendments could not have averted losses for consumers. To be sure, the results of this study suggest that any administrative change which shortens the NDA review process, decreases the attendant expense, and permits greater risk taking is likely to yield net benefits. But the clear mandate of the amendments for longer NDA review, more clinical testing expense, and more caution must ultimately limit the benefits. Therefore, if blame for the perversity of present drug regulatory policy is to be assessed, the most appropriate recipients will not be found in the FDA bureaucracy. They will be found in Congress and ultimately in its constituency.

APPENDIX

This appendix presents formally some of the theoretical and empirical results summarized in the text.

A Model of Drug Innovation

In this model each drug formula is treated as a homogeneous bit of nondepreciable therapeutic information. I assume that the demand for these bits by drug producers is derived from the expected size of the drug market. Specifically,

$$N_t^* = f(X_t^*), \tag{1}$$

where N_t^* = number of drug formulas producers wish to have available for marketing in year t,
and X_t^* = output of drugs producers anticipate in year t.

Producers must anticipate the size of the drug market, because production of new drugs entails a lengthy research and development (R&D) process. I assume that these anticipations are based on naive extrapolation of current levels of drug output and current output of an important complement, physicians' services. That is, if drug producers observe a decline in output of drugs or a decline in output of physicians' services, they will revise their estimate of future drug output downward, and reduce the resources committed to the new-drug development process. This reduced R&D commitment then translates into a reduced N* in the future. This may be expressed as

$$X_t^* = g(X_{t-j}, P_{t-j}), \tag{2}$$

and from (1)

$$N_t^* = h(X_{t-j}, P_{t-j}), \tag{3}$$

where P = output of physicians' services,
and j = gestation period for a new drug.

One would expect both the cost of producing drug formulas and demand for them to affect N*. For example, since much of this cost is labor expense for R&D personnel, the wages of R&D personnel relative to production personnel ought to influence the extent to which changes in X* are met from existing or new-drug formulas. Unfortunately, construction of an empirical counterpart to the relative wage variable is precluded by lack of continuous data on wages of R&D personnel, so the variable is omitted here. However, on the basis of fragmentary data, it appears this omission will not seriously bias the subsequent estimate of the effects of the 1962 amendments. There is no apparent upward trend or post-1962 increase in the relative wages of R&D and production personnel.[1]

It remains for us to specify how producers react to the demand for drug formulas in supplying new formulas in any marketing period (one year). The annual flow of new drugs may in this context be regarded as an attempt by producers to close the gap between the number of formulas they wish to have on the market and those already developed and marketed. I assume that the cost of closing this gap will rise with the rate at which it is closed, so that producers may not wish to eliminate the gap entirely in one marketing period. If this adjustment process is linear, we may then write

$$n_t^* = k (N_t^* - N_{t-1}), \qquad (4)$$

where n^* = number of new drug formulas producers wish to market, N_{t-1} = number of formulas available for marketing at the start of year t, and k = a constant coefficient of adjustment between zero and unity.

To implement (4), I assume that producers attain n^* on average, with deviations being random. I also assume that (3) is linear in form, so that when its right-hand side is substituted for N^* in (4) we get

$$n_t = a + b X_{t-j} + c P_{t-j} - k N_{t-1} + u, \qquad (4)'$$

where a, b, c = constants, and u = random variable.

The empirical counterpart to the dependent variable will be new chemical entities (NCEs). I therefore use Schnee's estimates that mean development time of a (pre-1962) NCE was about two years with standard deviation of one year in order to construct empirical counterparts to X_{t-j} and P_{t-j}. To conserve degrees of freedom, these counterparts employ three-term moving averages centered about t-2.

The least squares estimate of (4)' on 1948-1962 data is:

$$n_t = -2990.016 + 471.352 \, \overline{X}_{t-2} + 45.590 \, \overline{P}_{t-2} - .672 N_{t-1} \qquad R^2 = .80$$
$$\quad\quad\quad\quad (75.616) \quad\quad (32.142) \quad (.113) \quad\quad\quad (E1)$$

The standard error of estimate is 4.969; standard errors of coefficients are in parentheses. The variables are as follows:

n_t = number of NCEs introduced in t,[2]
$\bar{X}_{t-2}$ = log of three-year moving average of total number of out-of-hospital prescriptions sold (millions) centered about $t-2$,[3]
$\bar{P}_{t-2}$ = log of three-year moving average of personal consumption expenditures on physicians' services (million dollars) deflated by price index (1958 = 100) for these services and centered about $t-2$.[4]
N_{t-1} = cumulative number of NCEs introduced through $t-1$.[5]

The regression implies that size of the drug market is by far the more important of the two demand variables,[6] and that roughly two-thirds of the gap between N* and N is closed in any annual marketing period. Given the size of the coefficient of determination, this rather simple model is able to explain most of the variation in new chemical entity flows in the postwar period up to 1962. Indeed predicted values of E1 "track" actual pre-1962 flows much more closely even than the dotted line of Figure 1. This is especially true of the controversial 1959-62 decline in NCEs. The interested reader will find this relationship depicted in my article in Richard Landau, ed., *Regulating New Drugs* (Chicago: University of Chicago, Center for Policy Study, 1973).

I then use E1 to predict annual NCE flows in the post-1962 period, and compare these predictions with actual flows. The predicted flows are estimated by plugging post-1962 values of $\bar{X}$ and $\bar{P}$ and the implied values of N into E1;[7] they may be regarded as estimates of n in the absence of any change in the law. A plot of these estimates would correspond roughly with the dotted line in Figure 1. That is, they indicate that but for the 1962 amendments there would have been a gradual recovery in NCE introductions from the 1962 trough to a level in excess of forty per year for most of the 1960s. The average post-1962 predicted flow is forty-one per year. This is virtually identical with the average pre-1962 flow of forty. The mean difference between the predicted and actual post-1962 annual flows is over ten times its standard error and only in the transition year, 1963, is the difference much smaller than this average. These data imply that (a) the 1962 amendments significantly reduced the flow of NCEs and that (b) *all* of the observed difference between pre- and post-1962 NCE flows can be attributed to the 1962 amendments.

A Model for Estimating the Benefits and Costs of the 1962 Amendments

The model used in the estimates of Chapter IV and discussed informally in Chapter III can be stated as follows:

Write the true demand for new drugs (GHEN in Figure 3) as

$$p = f^* (q), \tag{5}$$

where p = price,
and q = quantity.

The true net benefit or consumer surplus from consuming new drugs, s, in any year, t, is then

$$s_t = \int_0^{q_t} f^* (q)dq - [p_t \, q_t]. \tag{6}$$

The first term on the right-hand side of (6) would correspond to OGHEC in Figure 3, and the second to OBDC. The actual demand at t (e.g., ADM) may be written

$$p = f^t (q), \tag{7}$$

so that (6) could be rewritten

$$s_t = \int_0^{q_t} f^* (q)dq - [f^t(q_t) \cdot q_t]. \tag{6}'$$

The assumption that f^* is, in the absence of regulation, revealed by experience leads to the empirical identification of f^* with f^T, where T is the time required for learning. I will assume further that f^T is attained linearly, so that,

$$\frac{df^t}{dt} = \frac{1}{T} (f^T - f^o), \tag{8}$$

and

$$f^t = f^o + t\frac{df^t}{dt} = \left(1 - \frac{t}{T}\right) \cdot f^o + \frac{t}{T} f^T. \tag{9}$$

This permits us to rewrite (6)' as

$$s_t = \int_0^{q_t} f^T (q)dq - \left[\left(1 - \frac{t}{T}\right) \cdot f^o (q_t)q_t + \frac{t}{T} f^T (q_t) \cdot q_t\right]. \tag{6}''$$

(Note that s can be negative, since $f^o \geqslant f^T$.)

New drugs yield benefits for more than a single year, so the stream of annual benefits must be discounted to yield the present value of that drug's net benefits (S). That is

$$S_t = \int_0^\infty s_t \, e^{-rt} \, dt, \tag{10}$$

where r is an appropriate discount rate.

94

This procedure will be modified in light of post-amendment experience. I will make the strong assumption that no learning by experience is required for f* to be revealed when the FDA approves any NDA under the amendments. Instead

$$F^* = F^o, \tag{11}$$

where F denotes a post-amendment demand curve. If F^T is smaller than F^o, this will be attributed to other market forces. Thus, for the post-1962 period, (6)'' would be simply

$$s_t = \int_0^{q_t} F^t(q)dq - [F^t(q_t) \cdot q_t]. \tag{12}$$

If $F^T \neq F^o$, this fact along with resulting price changes will be used to compute the "normal" growth or decline (g) in s:

$$g = \frac{1}{T} \ln \left(\frac{S_T}{S_o} \right), \tag{13}$$

so that (10) would be, simply,

$$S_t = s_o \int_0^\infty e^{-(r-g)t}dt = \frac{s_o}{r-g}. \tag{14}$$

Since $s_o \geq 0$, (14) can never be negative.

If $F^T \neq F^o$ and $F^o = F^*$, then this implies modification of the identification of f* with f^T. The modification to be employed will be

$$f^* = \min \left\{ \left[\frac{f^T}{f^o} \Big/ \frac{F^T}{F^o} \right] \cdot f^o, f^o \right\}. \tag{15}$$

That is, the differential growth in demand between the pre- and post-amendment period will be used to find f*, if demand did in fact grow more slowly (fall more rapidly) before the amendments. The f* of (15) will then be substituted for f^T in (6)''. Since f* also grows by g, (10) could then be written, for the pre-amendment period,

$$S_t = \int_0^T s_t e^{-rt} \, dt + e^{-rT} \frac{s_T}{r-g}. \tag{10}'$$

The 1962 amendments would then have positive net benefits if the value of S in (14) exceeded that in (10)'. This could occur if there were great losses from inefficacy, so that the first term on the right-hand side of (10)' were very small or negative. If, on the other hand, the amendments' restriction of privately produced information reduced s_o in (14) substantially compared with s_T in (10)', then S in (10)' would exceed that in (14), and there would be a net social cost for the amendments.

A Model for Estimating the Demand
for New Drugs, and the Net Benefits
and Costs of the 1962 Amendments

We wish to estimate a demand curve for new drugs from which estimates of consumer surplus can be derived. To do this, I assume that new-drug prescriptions within a therapeutic category are perfect substitutes. Then, the demand for new drugs may be written

$$q_{nt} = f(p_{nt}, p_{ot}, X_t), \qquad (16)$$

where t denotes a particular year
and q_n = number of prescriptions for new drugs in a therapeutic category per unit time,
p_n = the price per q_n,
p_o = the price of imperfect substitutes for new prescriptions,
X = a vector of all other factors affecting the demand for new drugs.

For simplicity, p_o is identified with the average price of prescriptions for old drugs in the same category. The vector X has two components: (1) all of the systematic nonregulatory factors apart from p_n and p_o that might affect the demand for new drugs (prices of complements, income, "tastes") are assumed to be reflected in total output of prescriptions in the therapeutic category (Q_T); (2) since the 1962 amendments may have changed the demand for new drugs, and since our data span the amendments, the presence or absence of the amendments (A) is included in X. It is assumed that (16) is homogeneous of first degree in all nonregulatory arguments and that there are random components of q_n, so that (16) may be rewritten:

$$\frac{q_{nt}}{Q_{Tt}} = f\left(\frac{P_{nt}}{P_{ot}}, A_t, u_t\right) \qquad (16)'$$

where u_t is a random variable.

In the subsequent empirical work (16)' is assumed to have the linear form:

$$\frac{q_{nt}}{Q_{Tt}} = a + b\frac{P_{nt}}{P_{ot}} + cA_t + u_t \qquad (17)'$$

with a, b and c constants; $a > 0$, $b < 0$, and the sign of c is uncertain. It is being assumed here that sellers set P_n/P_o in each period and offer to sell indefinitely large amounts at that price during the period. Variation in P_n/P_o is assumed to be determined largely by non-demand-related factors, such as costs, so that any empirical estimate of (16)' will largely reflect demand relationships.

Empirical Estimates. Estimates of (17) are in Table A-1. They employ data on therapeutic category market shares and relative prices for NCEs introduced in 1960-1962 and 1964-1969 for the year following introduction. The variable A is unity for each post-amendment observation and zero otherwise. Only those observations where significant NCE market penetration occurred (1 percent or more of category prescriptions and sales) are employed in the estimates. The categories are of widely varying size, and preliminary estimates revealed heteroskedastic residuals. As might be expected, residual variance decreased with category size. To restore homoskedasticity, Table A-1 shows weighted regression estimates of (17), with the ratio of total category prescriptions to total prescriptions for all drugs in the year of observation as the weight. Equation E2 reveals a significant negative relationship between market

Table A-1

ESTIMATED DEMAND CURVE FOR NEW CHEMICAL ENTITIES
(NCEs introduced 1960–1962, 1964–1969)

Equation and Dependent Variable	Constant	Coefficients and Standard Errors of:			R^2	S.E.
		P_n/P_o	q_n/Q_T	A		
E2: q_n/Q_T	.1188 (.0232)	−.0304 (.0132)		−.0510 (.0147)	.2885	.0687
E3: P_n/P_o	1.6922 (.1543)		−2.9084 (1.2588)	−0.3772 (.1501)	.8360	.6721
E4: q_n/Q_T	.3503 (.1550)	−.1871 (.0810)		−.0903 (.0519)		

Note: Sample consists of fifty-eight therapeutic categories, thirty-one in 1960–1962 and twenty-seven in 1964–1969.

Coefficients of E4 are simple averages of those in E2 and those implied by E3, and their standard errors are approximate upper bounds.

Definitions: q_n/Q_T = number of new prescriptions for NCEs divided by total number of new prescriptions for all drugs in therapeutic category in year following introduction of NCEs; P_n/P_o = average price per prescription for NCEs divided by average price per prescription for other drugs in category in year following introduction of NCEs (average price = dollar sales divided by number of prescriptions).

A = unity for 1965–70, zero otherwise.

R^2 = coefficient of determination.

S.E. = standard error of estimate (both for weighted data).

Standard errors are in parentheses below coefficients.

Source: R. A. Gosselin, Inc., *National Prescription Audit.*

shares attained by NCEs and their relative price, and a significant post-1962 decline in the level of demand. The elasticity of market share with respect to price (at sample means) suggested by E2 is .7, which indicates that consumers treat new and old drugs as poor substitutes for each other. The perceived consumer surplus from new drugs will be larger the less elastic is the demand for new drugs, and so too would the perceived loss of surplus resulting from the post-amendment decline in demand. However, in light of the measurement error in the price and quantity variables, it is risky to accept the estimates in E2 at face value. In particular, measurement error in P_n/P_o will lead to downward bias in the estimated demand elasticity. However, it is possible to obtain an upper bound to this elasticity by regressing price on quantity instead of quantity on price. This is done in E3, which suggests an elasticity fully ten times that of E2. It must be noted that the form of E3 contains the implausible implicit assumption that sellers of new drugs predetermine output and then find a price which clears the market of this output: E2 is therefore probably closer to the "truth" than E3. However, to keep the relevant estimates of consumer surplus conservative, I have assumed that the true values of the demand parameters lie exactly halfway between those in E2 and those suggested in E3. The resulting parameter estimates are shown in E4.

Equation (17) was also estimated for new drugs other than NCEs. The counterpart to (E2) was

$$\frac{q'_n}{Q_T} = \begin{matrix} .0515 \\ (.0357) \end{matrix} - \begin{matrix} .0049 \\ (.0299) \end{matrix} \frac{P'_n}{P_o} - \begin{matrix} .0251 \\ (.0095) \end{matrix} A, \qquad (E5)$$

where the prime refers to "other new drugs." The coefficients suggest a virtually inelastic demand curve which decreased after the amendments. Taken literally, this would mean a far more substantial perceived net benefit loss from the amendments for "other new" drugs than for NCEs. However, reversing the dependence of quantity on price generates an almost perfectly elastic demand curve which increased after the amendments. This would mean that consumers perceive no net benefits from "other new" drugs (they treat them as perfect substitutes for old drugs at prevailing prices), and that all of the value of the post-1962 increased demand for other new drugs is appropriated by price increases. Because they are derived from the same data, these conflicting interpretations as to the shape and location of the "other new" drug demand curve, imply substantial measurement error. While the true demand curve is surely neither perfectly elastic nor inelastic, the risk of error in using

98

the regression data to estimate demand parameters is much larger here than for NCEs.[8] In light of this risk, I have made what is here the most conservative assumption, that the true demand is perfectly elastic. This amounts to asserting that there is no perceived net benefit to consumers from a class of new drugs with total annual sales comparable to those of NCEs. I leave open the possibility that the 1962 amendments have produced net benefits for consumers of "other new" drugs.

The Perceived Loss of Consumer Surplus Resulting from the Amendments

The first ingredient in our estimate of the net benefits from the 1962 amendments is a gross cost: the decline in consumer surplus perceived by consumers upon their initial evaluation of information about new drugs. The higher pre-1962 evaluation of this information may reflect ignorance, so this gross cost of the amendments will have to be set off against gross benefits arising from reduced costs of learning from experience. At this stage, I am naively treating the initial demand, estimated by E4, as the "true" demand.

The general formula for calculating consumer surplus (an area such as ABD or GBH in Figure 3) with linear demand is

$$s = \frac{1}{2} (P_n^a - P_n) (q_n), \tag{18}$$

where the superscript "a" refers to the vertical intercept of the demand curve. In terms of the variables in E4, (18) would be:

$$s = \frac{1}{2} \left[\left(\frac{P_n}{P_o} \right)^a - \left(\frac{P_n}{P_o} \right) \right] \left[\frac{q_n}{Q_T} \right] \cdot P_o Q_T. \tag{18'}$$

An approximation to the total of (18)' over the whole drug market can then be obtained from the parameters and the appropriate sample means of E4 and the value of $P_o Q_T$ for categories with NCEs.[9] To provide comparable dollar values, $P_o Q_T$ is adjusted according to the size of the 1970 drug market. For this adjustment, the aggregate of $P_o Q_T$ for all categories with NCEs is divided by the aggregate for all sample categories in each year. Then the subperiod averages of this ratio (.235 before and .231 after the amendments) are multiplied by the 1970 value of $P_o Q_T$ for the whole drug market ($5.2 billion).[10] This permits (18)' to be evaluated at $51.9 million per year before the amendments and $9.9 million per year after the amendments; the perceived loss in consumer surplus resulting from the amendments is therefore $42.0 million annually for any year's flow of NCEs.[11] Since any year's NCEs will yield benefits over many years, the stream of these annual benefits must be converted to present values. For the moment, I treat the stream of benefits as a perpetuity with an unchanged average annual return. The return is, however, uncertain, because the (growth of) future demand for any set of new drugs and drugs in competition with that set will fluctuate. The appropriate discount rate for the stream of expected NCE benefits is the rate of return in activities with similarly risky rewards. I use a 10 percent annual rate of return, which roughly corresponds to the long-run average rate of return on investment in equities. This discount rate produces a perceived net loss to consumers of $420 million in each year that the amendments have been effective, or about 8 percent of total annual drug sales.[12]

This estimate must be modified in light of any more rapid decline (or slower growth) over time in the demand for pre-1962 as compared to post-1962 new drugs. The evidence in Table 2 in the text suggests that the demand for both types of new drugs has changed little over time. If it is assumed that such change as occurs is a change in intercept rather than in slope of demand, then Table 2 suggests that both pre- and post-amendment NCE demand have fallen slightly over time. In the pre-amendment period there is a fall in price with no increase in quantity, while the post-amendment decrease in quantity exceeds that expected from the small rise in price.[13] However, the post-1962 NCE demand curve falls by less than its pre-1962 counterpart. The data suggest that the vertical intercept of the post-1962 curve falls by .026 as against .087 for the pre-1962 curve. This .061 difference can be interpreted as the difference in intercept between the initial and true demand curves for NCEs before 1962, since it is assumed that all of the difference is the result of the greater incidence of inefficacious drugs prior to 1962. The implied true demand curve can then be used to estimate the true consumer surplus for NCEs (GHB in Figure 3) and the waste from initial ignorance of the NCEs' true value (HDE in Figure 3). Since the difference between initial and true demand is so small, it is not surprising that the difference between perceived and true surplus is small and the waste trivial. The estimated true surplus for pre-1962 NCEs in the first year after introduction is in fact $43.0 million instead of $51.9 million and the estimated waste only $0.4 million. The conclusion to which these data point is that the forgone consumer benefits of NCEs kept from the market by the amendments substantially exceed the waste avoided on inefficacious drugs.

Since ignorance is assumed to be dispelled by experience, this conclusion can only be strengthened by extending the relevant benefit and cost estimate beyond the first year in which any set of NCEs is marketed. Estimates were made on the assumption that both the true demand and the pre-1962 gap between initial and true demand decreased linearly for four years after NCEs were introduced. Prices and quantities for intermediate years were estimated by linear interpolation of the terminal values. The resulting estimates are in Table A-2. The pre-amendment surplus, net of waste, actually increased in spite of the small decline in true demand. This increase was the result of an increased dispersion of market shares not repeated for the post-1962 sample.[14] There is, consequently, a small decline over time in the surplus from post-1962 drugs.

Table A-2 also provides estimates of (10)′ and (14). These are derived by assuming that the pre-1962 growth in s_t ended abruptly at $t = 4$, and that the permanent subsequent growth in s has been that of the post-1962 series (about -2 percent per year). If the benefit streams are perpetual, the amendments are imposing a net loss on consumers of roughly \$400 million (\$491.0 − \$82.4 million) per year. If it is assumed that benefit streams from new drugs last for only fifteen years, the estimated net loss is about \$330 million annually.

Table A-2

ESTIMATED "TRUE" NET CONSUMER SURPLUS FOR ONE YEAR'S NCEs IN YEARS AFTER INTRODUCTION
(million dollars)

Item	Pre-Amendment NCEs	Post-Amendment NCEs
Years after introduction		
1	$ 42.6	$ 9.9
2	49.1	9.7
3	55.9	9.6
4	63.2	9.4
Present value of surplus stream for:		
(a) Perpetual stream	491.0	82.4
(b) 15-year stream	397.3	67.3

Note: True net consumer surplus is the estimated consumer surplus for the true demand curve less any waste for ineffective drugs. Waste is assumed zero for post-amendment NCEs. See text of appendix for method of calculation.

The Impact of Innovation on Average Drug Prices

For present purposes, I treat old and new drugs in the same therapeutic category as perfect substitutes for each other and focus on
the average price of all drugs in the category. I then measure the
net impact of drug innovation on this average. (It should be remembered that new drugs generally sell at a premium, so that, in the
absence of price rivalry, more innovation will increase this average.)
To measure the net impact, I first regress a time series of the
annual percentage change in average price per drug prescription
($\dot{p}_t$) in the pre-amendment period on the number of NCEs introduced
in each of the two preceding years ($n_{t-1,t-2}$). Since major initial sales
of any of the n_{t-1} are ordinarily attained in t, the coefficient of n_{t-1}
would reflect most of the inflationary impact of the new drug price
premium. If there is a lag in response of old-drug producers, the
coefficient of n_{t-2} would capture the major deflationary impact of
price rivalry. The regression fitted to data for 1952-62 is (standard
errors are below coefficients):

$$\dot{p}_t = 8.652 - .003n_{t-1} - .125n_{t-2} \qquad R^2 = .388 \qquad (E6)$$
$$(.006) \qquad (.058)$$

Since the coefficient of n_{t-1} is insignificant and that of n_{t-2} is significantly negative, the regression suggests that the dominant effect
of reduced drug innovation is reduced price rivalry. Specifically
E6 predicts that a permanent annual decline of twenty NCEs
would accelerate the change in drug prices by 2.5 percent per year.
However, while that magnitude of NCE decline has been experienced since 1962, the predicted price effect has not. Instead, there
has been a deceleration from the pre-1962 average of over 1 percent
per year. This might mean that the relationship in E6 is aberrant,
or that factors exogenous to that relationship have been holding drug
prices down since 1962.

To distinguish among these possibilities, I examine cross-section
data for the three years preceding the amendments. Exogenous
forces are assumed to affect all submarkets equally at any moment,
so the dependent variable is redefined as the deviation of the price
change for a category from the average price change for all categories in the same time period ($\dot{p}'$). Instead of the number of NCEs,
I use q_n/Q_T, as well as the market share of "other" new drugs
(q'_n/Q_T), as independent variables. The dependent variable is
measured over two years spanning the year subsequent to drug
innovations, which is the year used to measure the independent
variables. Hence, the coefficients of the independent variable reflect
both any immediate inflationary impact of the innovation and any

lagged competitive reaction. The resulting regression fitted to 153 observations (51 therapeutic categories, for 1960-62 innovations) is:

$$\dot{p}' = .329 - 13.230 \frac{q_n}{Q_T} - 1.216 \frac{q'_n}{Q_T} \quad R^2 = .036 \quad (E7)$$
$$\quad\quad\quad (5.625) \quad\quad (5.015)$$

While it is weak, the negative overall effect of NCEs on drug prices persists in the cross-section data, and the effect remains significant (non-NCE innovation has a neutral effect on drug prices). The magnitude of the predicted effect of reduced innovation on drug prices is, however, much smaller here than in E6. The average NCE share of category output declined by roughly 1½ percentage points, and in E7 this translates into an approximate .1 percentage point annual acceleration of average drug prices. This amounts to $5 million, given 1970 drug sales of about $5 billion. However, since the price increase is presumably permanent, there will be a continuing stream of these costs. The present value of this stream is $50 million, using a 10 percent discount rate. A similar $50 million cost stream is engendered each year that innovation is retarded.

A Model of the Relationship of Innovation to the Wealth of Drug Company Owners

This model attempts to capture the effects of the post-1962 reduction in drug innovation on the wealth of drug company owners. For simplicity, it is assumed that changes in wealth for drug stock investors as well as for investors in the general market are governed by changes in the expected growth in demand for drugs and other goods respectively. This can be expressed in linear form:

$$(\dot{w}_{dt} - \dot{w}_{mt}) = a(g_{dt} - g_{mt}) + u_t, \quad\quad\quad (19)$$

where $\dot{w}$ = rate of change of owner wealth, i.e., capital gains plus dividends divided by initial wealth,
g = change in the expected growth in demand for output,
u = random variable,
a = constant, and
the subscripts denote the drug industry (d) and the aggregate of all industries (m).

I assumed that investors revise their estimate of expected demand growth in light of the actual growth rate of output and the rate of innovation, both compared to the current expected rates. This implies that in linear form g can be expressed:

$$g_i = b_i (\dot{D}_i - \dot{D}_i^*) + c_i (n_i - n_i^*), \quad\quad\quad (20)$$

103

where $\dot{D}$, $\dot{D}^*$ = actual and expected rate of change in real output, respectively,

n, n* = actual and expected rate of innovation, respectively,

b, c = constants

i = d, m, and all variables are contemporaneous.

That is, g is zero unless there is unanticipated output growth or innovation. For simplicity, and to conserve degrees of freedom, I assume that $\dot{D}^*$ is a constant for both d and m, that $n_m = n_m^*$, and and $b_m \doteq b_d$. Further, I assume that n_d^* is constant within any subperiod.

These assumptions permit (19) to be written as

$$(\dot{w}_{dt} - \dot{w}_{mt}) = A + ab\,(\dot{D}_{dt} - \dot{D}_{mt}) \qquad (19)'$$
$$+ acn_{dt} + u_t$$

where

$$A = ab\,(\dot{D}^*_m - \dot{D}^*_d) - acn^*_d,$$

a constant in any subperiod.

We expect a and b to be positive, but are uncertain about the sign of c. If, for example, competitors lose more than an innovator gains, c would be negative. Moreover, the sign or magnitude of c may have been changed by the amendments. Since the behavior of c is crucial in determining the effect of the amendments, I resolve the uncertainty about it empirically.

The first step is to determine whether c was positive or negative prior to 1962. This is accomplished by estimating (19)' on pre-1962 data; this estimate is E8 in Table A-3. Growth of real drug output (including nonprescription items) and growth of real GNP are used as demand-change proxies, while n_d is measured by the number of NCEs. In view of the small number of drug companies for which wealth data are available (see note to Table A-3), considerable averaging is used to reduce the variance of wealth change measures. The wealth changes are measured from annual average market prices and yearly dividends (all assumed paid on June 30). Further, to prevent dominance of $\dot{w}_d$ by one or two unusually successful firms, it is assumed that an investor sells his holdings each year and then reinvests equal amounts in each drug company in the sample. The variable $\dot{w}_m$ is simply the wealth change for Standard and Poor's 425 Industrial Stock Price Index. The regression, in which the coefficient of the relative demand growth variable is significantly positive, indicates that increased

104

drug innovation produced increased wealth for drug owners before 1962. But the coefficient is insignificant, so we cannot rule out a neutral or even slightly negative effect of innovation on wealth.

It becomes more difficult to accept the hypothesis that the coefficient of n is positive when pre-1962 estimates of (19)′ are used to predict post-1962 wealth changes. If we assume that the coefficient is zero, in which case E9 is appropriate, and it is in fact positive, then extrapolation to the post-1962 period will over-predict wealth changes; we will fail to account for the decline in wealth resulting from reduced innovation. However, this extrapolation (columns (6) and (7) of Table A-3) yields wealth changes which are almost the same as the actual wealth changes. When the extrapolation is carried out accepting the positive coefficient of n, significant underprediction of actual wealth changes occurs. Part of this underprediction is no doubt the result of the naive implicit assumption that n* does not decline after 1962. However, the positive pre-1962 value of c can be made consistent with post-1962 data only by assuming perfect foresight. If the expected flow of NCEs (n*) is reduced by around twenty-five (the average difference between the pre- and post-1962 value of n) immediately in 1962, the intercept of E8 is increased sufficiently for that equation essentially to duplicate the average post-1962 prediction of E9. Even here, however, the correlation of the latter's predicted values with actual values (.60) exceeds that of E8 (.40). The best procedure then would seem to be to assume that c is zero, that innovation makes no net contribution to owner wealth after 1962. This conclusion seems strengthened when E9 is replicated on post-1962 data (E11 in Table A-3). Apart from some loss of explanatory power, the pre-1962 results are virtually duplicated. That is, the amendments have not restricted the ability of owners to share in any growth in drug demand.

One possible explanation for the failure of innovation to contribute to wealth after 1962 is suggested by E10, which replicates E8 on the later data. Here, the coefficient of n is negative, and, though it is again insignificant, one can only barely reject the hypothesis that this coefficient is less than the one in E8. This suggests that if pre-1962 innovation made a net contribution to owner wealth, the contribution has been reduced by the constraints in the amendments. This would be the case if the added costs of an innovation reduced the wealth gain to the innovating firm, so that the losses of competitors would become more important in the aggregate. However, the mean of the dependent variable is virtually the same in both subperiods, and its failure to decline with the coefficient

Table A-3

REGRESSION ESTIMATES OF EFFECT OF DRUG INNOVATION ON OWNER WEALTH

Estimate and Period	Constant (1)	Coefficients and Standard Errors of $\dot{D}_d - \dot{D}_m$ (2)	n (3)	R^2 (4)	S.E. (5)	Mean and Standard Errors of Extrapolations to 1962–71 for $(\dot{w}_d - \dot{w}_m)$ Estimated values (6)	Actual – estimated (7)
E8: 1949–61	−.1648 (.1298)	2.8331 (.9027)	.0034 (.0031)	.5307	.0899	−.0380 (.0167)	.0803 (.0256)
E9: 1949–61	−.0270 (.0334)	2.8672 (.9106)		.4741	.0907	.0378 (.0181)	.0044 (.0220)
E10: 1962–71	.1041 (.0892)	1.9338 (1.2323)	−.0058 (.0040)	.5078	.0688		
E11: 1962–71	−.0163 (.0361)	2.5901 (1.2252)		.3584	.0734		

Note: Dependent variable is $(\dot{w}_d - \dot{w}_m)$, where $\dot{w}_d$ is the log of simple average of current year's stock price plus dividends divided by last year's stock price for a sample of drug stocks (see below), and $\dot{w}_m$ is the log of current year's value for Standard and Poor's 425 Industrials plus dividends divided by last year's value.

$\dot{D}_d$ is the change in the log of real personal consumption expenditures on drugs.

$\dot{D}_m$ is the change in the log of real gross national product.

n is the average of current and previous year's NCEs (to center series about year end).

R^2 is the coefficient of determination, and S.E. is the standard error of estimate.

Column (6) is the average estimated value of dependent variable for 1962–71 using 1949–61 regression coefficients and 1962–71 actual values of independent variables.

Column (7) is the difference between actual 1962–71 values of dependent variable and those estimated for column (6).

Standard errors are in parentheses below coefficients and means.

Source: $\dot{w}_d$: Arnold Bernhard & Co., *Value Line Investment Survey* (New York, various issues). The drug stocks used in computing $\dot{w}_d$ were (initial year of appearance other than 1949 in parentheses): Abbott, American Home Products, Eli Lilly (1956), Merck, Parke-Davis (to 1969), Pfizer, Schering (1953), Searle (1951), Smith, Kline and French, Upjohn (1960). $\dot{w}_m$: Standard and Poor's Corp., *Security Price Index Record* (New York, 1972). $\dot{D}_d$, $\dot{D}_m$: U.S. Office of Business Economics, *National Income and Product Accounts of the United States, 1929–1965* (Washington, D. C.: Government Printing Office, 1966) and *Survey of Current Business* (Washington, D. C.: Government Printing Office, various issues). n: Paul de Haen, Inc., New York.

of n might reflect a smaller annual loss to those who compete with innovators. On this interpretation the absence of any overall wealth effect of the amendments is really the result of offsetting effects. The increased cost of each innovation has reduced wealth, but this has been partly offset by reduced innovation and then completely offset by the resulting reduction of competition in markets affected by innovation. This interpretation is generally consistent with previous findings that increased costs of innovation have not been reflected either in higher new-drug prices or in larger new-drug market shares, and that reduced innovation has tended to inflate prices of existing drugs.

The Value of Reduced Variability of Drug Company Owners' Wealth

The discussion in Chapter VI points out that the amendments have reduced the year-to-year fluctuation of the wealth of drug company owners and that, in light of their failure to suffer reduced returns, these owners can be presumed to have benefitted. A qualified estimate of the size of this benefit can be obtained by use of portfolio choice theory. I have treated the five firms for which we have continuous data (see text, Table 12) as representative of the drug industry. If an investor had concentrated his assets in the drug industry either before or after the amendments, his returns would have been superior to the market returns but he would have sacrificed the gains (if any) of portfolio diversification. The relevant questions here are these: (1) Given knowledge of the market return and its variability, how much better off than the investor in the "market" would the drug industry investor have been in light of the increased risk he would have incurred by not diversifying? (2) Would his gain have been greater after 1962? To answer these, I have used the following expression for the gain (E) resulting from the strategy of concentrating one's portfolio in the drug industry:

$$E = \left[D - N \right] - \left[(M - N) \cdot \left(\frac{S_D}{S_M} \right) \right], \qquad (21)$$

where D, M, N = rate of return on drug stocks (D), the general market (M), and a risk-free asset (N),

$S_{D,M}$ = standard deviation of D and M, respectively.

M, N and S_M are assumed known at the start of a multi-year investment period. A detailed rationale for (21) may be found elsewhere.[15]

Heuristically, the second term on the right-hand side of (21) represents the return (net of the non-risky return) available to an investor willing to incur the same variability provided by drug stocks if he merely holds an appropriate combination of other stocks and the non-risky asset. The appropriate combination may entail borrowing or selling short the non-risky asset. Thus, if drug stocks are twice as variable as the market, and the investor is willing to accept this degree of variability, he can attain a net return of 2 (M−N) on his equity by selling short an equal amount of the non-risky asset and investing the proceeds in a diversified portfolio of stocks. Now if D−N exceeds 2 (M−N), the investor is clearly better off precisely by this excess if he concentrated his equity in drug stocks: this excess is a bonus which he received without incurring added variability, and he would not have earned it if the market had correctly anticipated drug industry prospects when he made his investment.[16]

For the five drug stocks there was such a positive bonus in 1949-61: E was evaluated at +2.3 percent per year.[17] This increased to +4.3 percent per year in 1962-71, and all of the increase is due to reduced riskiness of drug stocks: S_D/S_M is actually less than unity (.84) after 1962. If one attributes all of the 2 percent annual improvement to the amendments, drug company investors have been made about 20 percent wealthier than investors in comparably risky assets. Converting this to a dollar magnitude presents formidable problems in view of the diversification of drug companies. But we have made the conservative assumption that the 20 percent bonus would apply to a "pure" domestic prescription drug company.[18] The average 1971 price-earnings ratio for drug stocks for which we have data was 30, and their total 1971 profits were 12 percent of total sales. I assume here that these ratios are applicable to the domestic prescription drug activities of these firms. Since 1971 manufacturer level sales of prescription drugs were about $3.5 billion, this assumption suggests that the owner wealth of the prescription drug industry was about $12.5 billion and that the amendment-induced bonus was about $2 billion. Such a bonus is equivalent to a perpetuity of $200 million per year at 10 percent.

The major qualification to this estimate arises from the fact that drug stock investors have continued to enjoy superior returns and reduced variability after the impact of the amendments on innovation became clear. One would expect that, when this impact became clear (say in the mid-1960s), the price of drug stocks would have been bid up so that subsequent investors would have obtained less risk at the cost of some return. However, the extent to which drug stocks outperformed the market was no different in 1967-71 from what it was in the previous five years. It is, of course, possible that it has taken the stock market longer than we have allowed to evaluate the impact of the amendments. If this is so, then my estimate of the benefits of the amendments to investors is reliable only if reduced risk is accompanied by commensurately reduced returns in the future. It should also be pointed out that my estimate suggests considerably larger effects of reduced innovation on the prices of old drugs than were estimated in Chapter IV. This may indicate that the estimate is too small, or, taken together with the persistence of the superior returns, it may indicate that these returns include effects of other unanticipated post-1962 factors, such as the advent of Medicare. Whatever the reason, it is relevant to note that year-to-year variability in drug sales has been smaller in the last decade than previously (see Figure 1) and this could be expected to have reduced the volatility of drug stock prices.

NOTES

NOTES TO CHAPTER I

[1] A good popular account of the Kefauver hearings and the subsequent congressional debate leading to the 1962 amendments may be found in Richard Harriss, *The Real Voice* (New York: Macmillan, 1964). The Kefauver Committee's elaboration of what follows is in U.S. Congress, Senate, Judiciary Committee, *Administered Prices: Drugs* (Washington, D. C.: Government Printing Office, 1961), especially Chapters 6-15.

[2] U.S. Senate, Judiciary Committee, *Administered Prices: Drugs*, p. 127. See also Chapters 6-15.

[3] See Harriss, *The Real Voice*.

NOTES TO CHAPTER II

[1] Schnee has estimated that the average development cost of a new chemical entity (NCE) before the amendments was more than triple that of a combination product; J. E. Schnee, "Research and Technological Change in the Ethical Pharmaceutical Industry" (Ph.D. dissertation, University of Pennsylvania, 1970), p. 77.

[2] J. Schmookler, *Invention and Economic Growth* (Cambridge, Mass.: Harvard University Press, 1966).

[3] Schnee, "Pharmaceutical Industry," p. 77. Development time is measured from initiation of clinical testing.

[4] See statement of H. E. Simmons, director, Bureau of Drugs, Food and Drug Administration, in U.S. Congress, Senate, Select Committee on Small Business, *Competitive Problems in the Drug Industry*, pt. 23 (Washington, D. C.: Government Printing Office, 1973).

[5] William Wardell, "The Drug Lag: An International Comparison," mimeo. (University of Rochester School of Medicine, 1972).

[6] For reasons given subsequently, these data exclude two important drug categories (diuretics and oral contraceptives) which were essentially invented just before 1960, but where substantial post-1962 innovation took place. Their inclusion would bring the post-1962 annual NCE share up to 1.18 percent compared to 1.77 percent for the pre-1962 period. It would be risky, though, to conclude from this last comparison that there is a persistent tendency to increase output per NCE. The effect of these few major innovations is concentrated in the first triplet of the post-1962 years, which implies that they are a "spin-off" of pre-amendment innovation. The average annual NCE share for 1967-70 is a mere 0.36 percent. More important perhaps, no wholly new drug category has appeared since 1962 which has produced innovations that now seem capable of duplicating the impact of diuretics and oral contraceptives. The safest conclusion to draw here would be that the decline in number of new drugs has been roughly matched by a decline in their output.

[7] J. M. Jadlow, "The Economic Effects of the 1962 Drug Amendments" (Ph.D. dissertation, University of Virginia, 1970), p. 174.

[8] Private communication from the Food and Drug Administration to the author.

[9] H. Clymer, "The Changing Costs and Risks of Pharmaceutical Innovation," in *The Economics of Drug Innovation*, ed. J. D. Cooper (Washington, D. C.: American University, 1970), pp. 115-116.

[10] Wardell, "The Drug Lag," and "Introduction of New Therapeutic Agents in the United States and Great Britain: An International Comparison," mimeo. (University of Rochester School of Medicine, 1972).

NOTES TO CHAPTER III

[1] The reader should not treat that discussion as an analysis of the pharmacological competence of the FDA. Such an analysis would be presumptuous and could easily lead to the erroneous conclusion that the effect of the amendments on consumer welfare depends solely on who administers them. Therefore, the relative pharmacological competence of the FDA and other expert groups is not discussed here.

[2] Where the extra information would have been worthwhile the price of a properly defined drug-information bundle is increased by the quantitative restriction, but the price per pill falls. Consumers simply pay a little less for a much inferior product package.

[3] The effects on research and development cost may be estimated from a time series of real research and development (dollar expenses divided by the GNP price deflator) per "NCE equivalent." An "NCE equivalent" is defined as 1 NCE + .30 new combination product + .16 new dosage form; the weights are Schnee's estimates of the relative research and development cost of different new-drug types ("Pharmaceutical Industry," p. 77). According to Schnee's estimates of development time for these types of new drugs, the number of NCE equivalents appropriate to any year's research and development is a three-year moving average centered about one (new combinations and dosage forms) or two (NCEs) years later. Before 1960, real research and development per NCE equivalent was increasing at 14.8 percent per year (the correlation coefficient with time being + .96). When this rate of increase is extrapolated beyond 1962, estimates of real research and development per NCE equivalent are obtained which are consistently below the actual values. For 1965-69, the extrapolated values average about half the actual values: that is, the amendments appear to have doubled the research and development costs per NCE. These extra research and development costs come to between $5 and $10 million per NCE equivalent, or roughly a year's sales for a fairly successful NCE. Even if sales remained this large forever, the amortization charge for this extra research and development would raise unit costs by at least the rate of interest which the developer could obtain by investing the funds elsewhere.

NOTES TO CHAPTER IV

[1] To minimize the effect of errors in categorization, minor therapeutic categories (fewer than 1 million prescriptions in most years sampled), and minor new drugs (fewer than 1 percent of all category prescriptions or sales) are excluded from the sample. This is done because we wish to examine the behavior of the typical new drug within the typical category. Where a new drug gets an unusually small share of a category, it is presumed to be related in demand to only a part of the category, so that for this drug the category is too comprehensive. If the new drug is related in demand to drugs outside its defined category, the resulting exaggeration of its importance will be most

serious if the defined category is small. I have also excluded categories where new drugs account for half of prescriptions or sales in the current or any of the three preceding years. This kind of innovation essentially creates a new category, and the new drugs are presumed to have no good substitute or none that are really "old" drugs.

[2] This market life is at least a decade: the average 1970 market share of NCEs introduced in 1960 is roughly equal to that in 1961 or 1964.

[3] D. D. Jones and J. F. Follman, Jr., *Health Insurance and Prescription Drugs* (New York: Health Insurance Association of America, 1971), pp. 99-100.

[4] Replication of these tests in the future may show more consistency among experts. The National Academy of Sciences is reviewing the efficacy of all pre-1962 drugs, and the FDA is empowered to remove inefficacious old drugs from the market. Illinois, however, has alerted physicians that drugs deemed ineffective by the NAS review may be deleted from the formulary before any FDA action. See *Drug Manual for Physicians* (Springfield, Illinois: Department of Public Aid, 1971).

[5] The following description of a group-I drug illustrates the kind of judgments made. "Results of clinical studies to date indicate that [drug] may be useful in treating [list of conditions], but data are insufficient to permit comparison of its effectiveness with that of recommended doses of other [drugs]. The usefulness of [drug] in [list of other conditions] has not been proved."

A generous interpretation of this might be that the drug is clearly effective for some conditions and possibly others. I made the pessimistic assumption that doctors are prescribing the drug only for those conditions where usefulness has not been proved, or that the apparently incomplete clinical data are too optimistic.

[6] There are two sub-classes in II: (1) those labeled "as effective" as some other specified drug or any other drug in the therapeutic category, and (2) those "less effective" than some other drug or group of drugs. A drug labeled "as effective" in the drug evaluations is in group II if the average cost of a prescription in the year following its introduction exceeds that of the specified alternative; all "less effective" drugs are in group II.

[7] Waste each year was divided by total drug sales that year, and the average of this quotient in each subperiod was multiplied by 1970 total drug sales to obtain these figures.

[8] Limitation of our sample to NCEs may, however, be important here. The AMA is extensively critical of combination drugs, generally on the ground that only one component affects a given symptom and that "rational" prescribing requires the physician to select the appropriate component. Any waste calculation for combination products based on *AMA Drug Evaluations* conclusions would be extremely difficult. The differences between the cost of the appropriate NCE bought separately and as part of a combination would have to be set against the cost of more extensive diagnosis and the added cost of separate prescribing where each part of a combination has some expected benefit.

[9] If $17.3 million of waste decreases by something like the 15 percent per year implied here, the present value of the waste issuing from one year's NCEs is $69 million (17.3/[.10 + .15]) rather than $173 million, and the improvement resulting from the amendments is $56 million rather than $139 million.

[10] The sixteen "ineffective" pre-1962 drugs in our sample had an average initial market share of 8.7 percent and their average relative price was 1.16. For all pre-amendment NCEs in our sample, these figures are 7.5 percent and 1.26.

[11] From 1947 to 1962, the FDA budget, deflated by the price index for general government output, rose 6.6 percent per year. In the two subsequent years, this accelerated to 18.0 percent. The 1964-70 growth rate was 4.4 percent. If we assume that the pre-1962 growth rate would have been maintained if the

amendments had not been enacted, the 1970 budget would have been about $59 million, or $7 million lower than the actual 1970 budget. Alternatively, if we compound the 1962 budget at the slower post-1964 growth rate, the estimated 1970 budget is $15 million below the actual.

NOTES TO CHAPTER V

[1] For a discussion of some of the relevant issues, see E. J. Mishan, "Evaluation of Life and Limb: A Theoretical Approach," *Journal of Political Economy*, vol. 79 (1971), pp. 687-705.

[2] For example, if one treats society as including everyone but the victim, the monetary loss of his death is his expected future wealth contribution, that is, his earnings minus his consumption.

[3] The amendments cannot, for example, be reasonably expected to reduce materially adverse effects of long-term use, since they add only a few years time to the clinical testing process.

[4] It should be pointed out that I am using a 10 percent discount rate for symmetry with previous and subsequent work, and that this rate understates the saving. An appropriate discount factor would be lower by the expected annual growth of population and per capita income. In this case, however, the understatement is mitigated by the fact that the highest incidence of aplastic anemia is among the very young and very old, who have a lower present value of earnings than any appropriate national average.

[5] The reader may verify this assertion by consulting the exceedingly critical anecdotal accounts of drug safety in Morton Mintz, *By Prescription Only* (Boston: Houghton-Mifflin, 1967).

[6] See U.S. Congress, Senate, Select Committee on Small Business, *Competitive Problems in the Drug Industry*, pt. 4 (Washington, D. C.: Government Printing Office, 1968), pp. 1515-54, and D. M. J. Bennett, "Liability of Manufacturers of Thalidomide to the Affected Children," *Australian Law Journal*, vol. 39 (1965), pp. 256-268.

[7] An indication of how extreme this assumption is may be found in M. L. K. Pringle and D. O. Fiddes, *The Challenge of Thalidomide* (London: Longmans, 1970).

[8] This is roughly the present value at birth of the lifetime earnings of 9,500 males and an equal number of females, where future earnings are discounted at 10 percent. More detail on the method of calculation may be found in the note to Table 8.

[9] The costs of increased development time are measured in Chapter IV through effects on drug prices and output. The additional time required to meet the proof-of-efficacy and testing requirements of the amendments results in loss of some return on the capital invested in R&D. Part of this cost is presumably reflected in higher new drug prices and fewer new drugs, and therefore in reduced consumer benefits.

[10] Burton Weisbrod, *Economics of Public Health* (Philadelphia: University of Pennsylvania Press, 1961). In addition, the average length of stay in TB hospitals in the late 1940s was about eight months. Since hospital admittees could be expected to have had the disease for some time prior to admission, Weisbrod's estimate seems reasonable.

[11] This loss should be netted against savings on purchase of the drugs, but these are trivial. The earliest data I have are for 1955, during which manufacturer shipments of all TB drugs were under $10 million.

[12] See L. Goodman and A. Gilman, *The Pharmacological Basis of Therapeutics* (New York: Macmillan, 1965), p. 176.

[13] Ibid., pp. 163, 177.

[14] I assume lifetime consumption of something over ten phenothiazine prescriptions per year at 1970 retail prescription prices. (These prices cannot be printed here.) The $600 estimate does not allow for any impact on drug prices from the 1971 expiration of the patent on chlorpromazine.

[15] This retail value is slightly under $250 million. The drugs include all phenothiazines and any others mentioned as antipsychotic agents in *AMA Drug Evaluations*, Chapter 29.

[16] This may still overstate the hypothetical cost of the 1962 amendments. Some of the overall tranquilizer benefits are attributable to the variants of chlorpromazine. The information produced for the chlorpromazine NDA might be expected to reduce the time required for approval of NDAs for the variants.

[17] Burton Weisbrod, "Costs and Benefits of Medical Research: A Case Study of Poliomyelitis," *Journal of Political Economy*, vol. 79 (1971), pp. 527-544.

[18] American Medical Association, *Report of the Commission on the Cost of Medical Care*, vol. 3 (Chicago: American Medical Association, 1964), pp. 29-46.

[19] Detail of the calculations is available from the author.

[20] American Medical Association, *Report of the Commission on the Cost of Medical Care*, pp. 13-14.

[21] To put these figures in perspective, about 750,000 succumb annually to the leading cause of death (heart disease) and 30,000 to the tenth leading cause (cirrhosis of the liver). Among common sources of disability, some diseases that cost over 100,000 man-years of productivity annually and are not leading causes of death are psychoses, bone diseases (for example, arthritis) and digestive system disorders (for example, ulcers and appendicitis). See U.S. Public Health Service, *Estimating the Cost of Illness*, Health Economics Series no. 6 (Washington, D. C.: Government Printing Office, 1966).

[22] That is, the annual return on the more than $3 billion capital value loss from delay.

[23] This improvement began about 1950 for both diseases. From 1900-1950, the death rate from cancer was increasing at about 1½ percent per year and that from heart disease at about ¾ percent per year. Since 1950, the heart disease death rate has stopped rising, while the rate of increase for cancer has been halved.

[24] President's Commission on Heart Disease, Cancer and Stroke, *Report to the President*, vol. 2 (Washington, D. C.: Government Printing Office, 1965).

[25] I am indebted to Scott Dittrich for assistance with these computations.

[26] This procedure produces a virtually constant total death rate for both diseases, which for cancer may be somewhat optimistic.

[27] According to a 1965 study, for each cancer and heart disease death approximately one man-year of earnings was lost by absence from the labor force of those alive but disabled by the disease (President's Commission on Heart Disease, Cancer and Stroke, *Report*, vol. 2). Therefore, on the assumption of an unchanged ratio of morbidity to mortality, one year's cohort median income is used as one component of the morbidity cost per death. The same study reports total 1962 expenditures for hospitals, nursing, and physician services for each disease (*Report*, vol. 2, p. 449ff.). For each expenditure category, I divided these totals by the number of 1962 deaths and multiplied the quotient by the ratio of the 1970 price index to the 1962 price index. The sum of these figures for each disease is an estimate of 1970 disease treatment costs per death. These are $4,897 for heart disease and $6,639 for cancer, and are the second component of morbidity cost per death in each cohort.

[28] My estimate for the first-year mortality reduction for TB drugs is about 4,300, compared with the six-year total of 753 deaths due to chloramphenicol (Table 6), both on a 1970 population base.

NOTES TO CHAPTER VI

[1] More precise measures of drug stock variability relative to the market are as follows:

(1) The standard deviation of annual returns to an investor holding the five drug stocks listed in Table 12 divided by the standard deviation of returns to Standard and Poor's Industrials is 1.21 for 1949-61 and .84 for 1962-71.

(2) The standard deviation of the difference between the return on each of the five drug stocks and the return on Standard and Poor's Industrials is:

	1949-61	1962-71
Abbott	19.8%	15.5%
American Home Products	16.6	14.3
Merck	26.2	14.0
Pfizer	24.0	18.7
Smith, Kline and French	25.4	15.1

(3) The annual standard deviation of returns among the five companies averages 19.3 percent for 1949-61 and 14.5 percent for 1962-71.

All three measures indicate that drug stocks have become less volatile since 1962.

[2] See, for example, M. C. Jensen, "Risk, the Pricing of Capital Assets and the Evaluation of Investment Portfolios," *Journal of Business*, vol. 142 (1969), pp. 167-247.

NOTES TO EPILOGUE

[1] "Frustrating Drug Advancement," *Newsweek*, January 8, 1973.

[2] The hearing proceedings are in U.S. Congress, Senate, Select Committee on Small Business, *Competitive Problems in the Drug Industry*, pt. 23 (Washington, D. C.: Government Printing Office, 1973).

[3] Ibid., p. 9422.

[4] Ibid., p. 9424.

[5] See *Wall Street Journal*, April 8, 1971. The 1962 amendments empower the FDA to remove from the market those pre-1962 drugs it deems ineffective. The NAS-NRC review is designed to assist the FDA in implementing this provision.

[6] J. M. Jondrow, "A Measure of the Monetary Benefits and Costs to Consumers of the Regulation of Prescription Drug Effectiveness" (Ph.D. dissertation, University of Wisconsin, 1972).

[7] Senate, Select Committee on Small Business, *Competitive Problems*, pt. 23, p. 9448.

[8] William Wardell, "Therapeutic Implications of the Drug Lag," mimeo. (University of Rochester Medical Center, 1973).

NOTES TO APPENDIX

[1] The Bureau of Labor Statistics reports that from 1961 to 1970 the average annual salary of chemists (a prototypical form of research labor) rose by 50.2 percent (*National Survey of Professional, Administrative, Technical and Clerical Pay*, various issues). This corresponds closely to the 52.6 percent rise in average hourly earnings of drug industry production workers (Bureau of Labor Statistics, *Employment and Earnings*, various issues). Data from the U.S. *Census of Population* show that from 1949 to 1959 median annual income

of chemists rose by 63.8 percent while that of "natural scientists" rose 74.0 percent. In the same period, BLS data show a 55.8 percent increase in average hourly earnings for drug production workers (*Employment and Earnings*). Taken together the data imply a slightly more favorable labor cost environment for research after 1962 than before. However, annual earnings of research personnel could have been unduly depressed by the 1949 recession, and the safest conclusion would be that no obvious labor cost inducement to substitute production for research activity can explain any of the post-1962 decline in new drug innovation.

[2] Paul de Haen, Inc., *de Haen Nonproprietary Name Index*, vol. 8 (New York: Paul de Haen, Inc., 1971).

[3] *American Druggist*, various issues.

[4] U.S. Office of Business Economics, *National Income and Product Accounts of the United States, 1929-1965* (Washington, D. C.: Government Printing Office, 1966), and *Survey of Current Business*, various issues.

[5] Paul de Haen, Inc., *de Haen Nonproprietary Name Index*; the cumulation is begun from 1945, so that N_{t-1} is, in fact, the "true" number of chemical entities developed to $t-1$ minus a constant (the number developed to 1945). This difference between N_{t-1} and the "true" value will affect only the intercept of the regression estimate of (4)'.

The cumulation procedure assumes no depreciation of the stock of chemical entities. In fact, old chemical entities are sometimes withdrawn from the market, but this does not imply that the knowledge embodied in them has worn out. That knowledge is nondepreciable, and we treat each NCE as a net addition to the stock of knowledge.

[6] A given percentage change in X increases the demand for chemical entities by more than ten times that of the same percentage change in P.

[7] That is, N is computed by adding the post-1962 predicted values of n to N_{1962}.

[8] The standard error of the average of the two estimated price coefficients is so large that it fails to rule out either perfectly elastic or perfectly inelastic demand.

[9] The appropriate sample means are the root mean square of q_n/Q_T and its associated P_n/P_o. Use of the simple average of q_n/Q_T understates aggregate surplus; surplus for below average q_n/Q_T is overvalued by less than the undervaluation of surplus for above average q_n/Q_T.

[10] This is essentially the value of prescription sales at retail outlets as estimated from *National Prescription Audit* data. The *NPA* reports estimated sales at the manufacturer's level, which they estimate at .48 of retail value. I have excluded drug sales to hospitals, since these data are not used to estimate the relevant demand curve. Such sales are roughly one-third of those of manufacturer sales to the retail market, so our surplus estimates may be considerably understated.

[11] The data underlying these estimates are as follows:

Variable	Pre-Amendment Period	Post-Amendment Period
(P_n/P_o) [a]	1.872	1.390
(P_n/P_o)	1.199	1.094
(q_n/Q_T)	.1259	.0554

These data assume that only the height and not the slope of the demand curve has changed. When E4 was reestimated to allow for change in slope, the resulting difference in surplus estimates increased. However, since the change in slope is insignificant, it is ignored here.

[12] The reader should keep clear the distinction between two benefit streams affected by the amendments, the annual benefits derived from the stream of

NCEs and the stream of benefits derived from any one year's NCEs. The reduction in the second is $420 million, and this is repeated annually.

[13] From E4, the (1.221-1.184) rise in price should have reduced the post-1962 market share by only .007 rather than by the .011 actually observed.

[14] The increased dispersion raises the root-mean-square market share, which is the quantity at which surplus is evaluated, even though the arithmetic average market share is unchanged.

[15] See M. C. Jensen, "Risk, the Pricing of Capital Assets and the Evaluation of Investment Portfolios."

[16] One might wish to assume that investors do not concentrate on drug stocks, but merely hold them as part of a diversified portfolio. Equation (21) will then be inappropriate, since diversification can reduce some of the risk implied by a high S_D. The term (S_D/S_M) can be expressed as (B/r), where B is the "systematic" risk of drug stocks and r is their correlation with the market. The B component is the average change in drug stock returns for each percentage point change in the "market" return, and it is B rather than the total (S_D/S_M) which may be of interest to the fully diversified investor. His diversification eliminates that risk resulting from the fact that r is less than one. Thus, for fully diversified investors, the discussion would focus on a form of (21) with B substituted for (S_D/S_M). It turns out, however, that r is the same (.63) for both subperiods, so that the reduction of S_D without loss of return has the same favorable implications for the welfare of fully diversified and specialized drug stockholders.

[17] D, M, S_D, S_M are computed from the continuously compounded annual wealth changes in the five-drug stock series and Standard and Poor's 425 Industrials. For 1949-61, N is set equal to 2.2 percent, the approximate yield of a 13-year U.S. Treasury Bond. For 1962-71, N = 3.9 percent, the approximate 1961 yield of a 10-year Treasury Bond.

[18] Since there is presumably no bonus on nonprescription drug activities, the bonus would have to exceed 20 percent on the value of prescription drug activities for a diversified company's value to rise 20 percent.

DATE DUE